KNOWS NO BOUNDARIES,

AND NEITHER SHOULD YOUR RINGS.

EXTRAORDINARY JEWELLERY FOR UNCOMMON PEOPLE

WWW.DEBRAFALLOWFIELD.COM

debrafallowfieldjeweller

THE TEAM

EDITOR & CO-FOUNDER
Tara Baker

CREATIVE DIRECTOR & CO-FOUNDER
Arlia Hassell

CONTRIBUTING PHOTOGRAPHERS
April Evelyn Photography, Brogan Jessup Photography, Calder Photography, Chasewild, Cori Taylor Photography, Erin Fraser Fox & Kin, Henry Tieu Photography, Kenz & Nick Photography Lightsmith Images, McKenzie Bigliazzi Photography, Rainwater Photography, Samantha Lowe Photo, The Nook

FRONT COVER IMAGE
Calder Photography
www.calderphoto.com

BACK COVER IMAGE
McKenzie Bigliazzi Photography
www.mckenziebigliazzi.com

EDITORIAL CONTRIBUTIONS
Andi, Emily Chelsea Jewelry, Kayla, Fairina Cheng

SUBMISSIONS
www.dancingwithher.com/submityourstory

ADVERTISING & WHOLESALE ENQUIRIES
partnerships@dancingwithher.com

DANCING WITH HER
P.O. Box 609
Coolangatta, QLD, 4225
Australia

JOIN OUR COMMUNITY
www.dancingwithher.com

facebook.com/dancingwithher
instagram.com/dancingwithher
pinterest.com/dancingwithher

Dancing With Her acknowledges the Australian Aboriginal and Torres Strait Islander peoples of this nation. We acknowledge the people of the Bundjalung Nation whose Land on which our company is located and where we primarily conduct our business. We pay our respects to Ancestors and Elders, past, present and emerging. Dancing With Her is committed to honouring Australian Aboriginal and Torres Strait Islander peoples unique cultural and spiritual relationships to the land, waters and seas and their rich contribution to society.

© 2019 Dancing With Her®
All rights reserved. Reproduction in whole or part without permission is strictly prohibited.

010
THINGS WE LOVE

012
ASHLEIGH & BRI-ANNE

020
ANDI & TOVAH: A PROPOSAL

024
THE REAL COST OF WEDDING JEWELS

028
CELESTE & ERICA

036
MARRIED TO A MAN, IN LOVE WITH A WOMAN

038
EMILY & LIZ

047
THE RISE OF MICRO WEDDINGS

048
ALYSHA & MICHAELA

057
PLANNING A MARRIAGE

058
ANNE & KIRA

066
MEET AMANDA AFTON PHOTOGRAPHY

068
DEE & SARAH

074
HOW TO SAVE YOUR WEDDING PARTY MONEY

076
THE PROPOSALS

080
LOVE IN THE MOUNTAINS

084
CYDNEY & JORDAN

092
LOVE FREELY, LOVE WHOLLY

097
HOW TO END YOUR WEDDING WITH A BANG

098
KATIE & TAYLOR

107
THE LIST

117
HONEYMOONS

LIGHTSMITH IMAGES

Brisbane wedding + elopement photographer

www.lightsmithimages.com.au

HELLO

When we decided to hit publish on the very first edition of our print magazine, our nerves were through the roof. We had no idea what to expect. We didn't know if anyone would buy the magazine, we had no idea if we would ever get the opportunity to print again.

But here we are. Welcome to Volume 6, lovers.

We still have all those nerves every time we send another one of our babies out into the wild, but they're probably nothing on the nerves you'll feel the week/day before your wedding day. Wedding planning is a wild ride. There will be ups and downs, and almost everyone will get to a point where they will want to throw in the towel ("it's just a piece of paper" is undoubtedly a phrase that has been thrown around in our own wedding planning journey). However, we hope that once you've read through these eight incredible weddings & love tales, you'll see that your wedding is worth any bit of angst that went into making it happen. We hope that amongst these pages, you'll find some of the very best wedding vendors who not just support your wedding, but celebrate it wholeheartedly.

No two weddings are ever alike- and quite frankly, that's one of our favorite things about them. Each wedding inside this issue is unique, from Alysha & Mic's industrial evening affair to Deanna & Sarah's beach romantic beach elopement.

We get the opportunity to speak with Kayla, who first fell for her now fiance, Megan, while she was married to a man. Her vulnerability will touch your heart.

Inside you'll also find one of the most romantic letters we've ever read [hint: it ends in a marriage proposal!], and we'll take you on that romantic beachside honeymoon to the white sands of The Whitsundays, Australia, that you've always dreamt about.

We hope you love this edition as much as we loved putting it all together for you.

Love,
Arlia & Tara

Producing minimal and refined stationery for the modern couple, Sunday Nude was born from a love of design and luxury stationery.

From save the dates and invitations right through to day of and signage, Sunday Nude works closely with you to translate your vision into reality- making all your minimalism dreams come to life.

Our pick - this minimal table number, proving that there is beauty in simplicity. Oh, and we also love the place cards. And, the invitations… okay, we'll take it all.

www.sundaynude.com

Sick to the post of correcting people on your pronouns? These little pins [they're the size of a quarter!] make the statement for you. They come in a selection of different pronoun options and the team at Gamut donate $1 from every pin sold to Camp Aranu'tiq, a nonprofit program serving transgender & gender-variant youth and their families.

www.gamutpins.bigcartel.com

Velvet vintage-inspired personalized ring boxes, yes, please! These Voeu Du Coeur creations are made by a women-led team that uses the world's finest fabrics [think fabrics from Valentino, Armani, Gucci and Alberta Ferretti] sourced from France and Italy to create these gorgeous heirloom boxes to keep your wedding jewels safe.

www.voeu-du-coeur.com

Classique Monogram Wax Seals are the perfect way to elevate your wedding stationery. These ones are individually stamped by our artisans to give you the traditional, handmade look and feel. There's even a Recycled Edition for eco-conscious lovers that features 100% repurposed wax — made in limited runs.

www.artisaire.com

These artisan KARMME scents are really beautiful. Sparkling blooms introduce a warm heart of spiced lilies with a gentle linger of honey, musk, and sandalwood.

Each Eau de Parfum, that is created in Sydney, is presented in a French-made bottle and nestled inside KARMME's signature indigo blue box.

Maybe it's a gift for your bride to be, perhaps it's a gift for your wedding party, or maybe it's a little, much deserved, treat just for you.

www.karmme.com.au

We love nothing more than to see where our children [aka our magazines] end up in the world! Want to win the very next issue delivered to your doorstep? Just share an image of this issue of Dancing With Her Magazine to Instagram, tag us and use the hashtag #dancingwithher to enter!

Who knows, maybe your image will make it into Volume 7!

The competition will close January 31st, 2020.

IG / @dancingwithher

Lockets are ancient amulets of love that carry good luck and ward off all that is less than love, and we're obsessed with this one. Featuring a little sapphire inside, the Meri Locket leaves you to fill it with the one you desire, the one you hold close, the one you choose every single day.

Their entire collection is perfect for your wedding and everyday wear. And, while the locket might be our favorite piece, we also love the rich cultural influences that adorn each ring, necklace, earring, and bracelet.

These jewels are, of course, made from sustainably sourced materials - good for the planet, something to treasure for all eternity.

Made in Australia's most easterly town, Byron Bay, these beauties can be shipped around the globe.

www.templeofthesun.com.au

We've always made it clear that we love an individual who isn't afraid to do exactly what they want, and what makes them most comfortable on their wedding day. For some people getting married, that's a huge princess ball gown, and for others, it might be a three-piece black tux with a bolo tie. And, for the lover who just dreams of an off the shelf garment that they feel comfortable in, this Maje romper might just be perfect.

We also envisage that a romper like this might be great for your bach party or even as outfits for the wedding party.

The best part; it's only $415, and it is absolutely something that you'll be able to wear more than just once!

www.maje.com

WIN! WIN! WIN!

Neons are the way to our hearts. Want to have this heart neon by Neon Poodle for your walls at home?

Competition is open to residents across the world and we've made it super simple to enter- just head to www.dancingwithher.com/win to enter.

www.neonpoodle.com.au

SUITS FOR QUEER BODIES: HERE ARE FOUR PLACES TO GET SUITED UP

01
SHANE AVE

Based in Australia, but shipping across the globe, this queer owned suit company make having a custom suit made easy.

IG / @shane.ave

02
TUX COUTURE

If a wedding day tux is your vibe, these are custom made in New Jersey- if you can dream it up, this crew can bring it to life.

IG / @tuxcouture

03
SHARPE SUITING

Wedding suits that are customized perfectly to your style and personality- plus Sharpe Suiting donates suits to LGBTQ+ youth- yes!

IG / @sharpesuiting

04
BINDLE & KEEP

Every single suit is hand-cut and created to fit your own specific measurements and their prices and processes super transparent.

IG / @bindleandkeep

ASHELIGH & BRI-ANNE

PHOTOGRAPHY BY ERIN FRASER
www.efraserphoto.com

PEMBERTON, CANADA

There were two proposals.

The first one was on the beautiful Galiano Island in British Columbia. Together Ashleigh and Bri-anne climbed Mount Galiano and surrounded by ocean views [and a nearby beehive], Bri-anne asked Ashleigh to marry her. Ashleigh was taking photos of the view and turned around to find Bri-anne down on one knee.

About a month later, Ashleigh proposed to Bri-anne. She scattered keepsakes from through the years of their relationship around the apartment. When Bri-anne returned home from work, she was surprised to find Ashleigh down on one knee.

They both said yes.

When it came to dress shopping, the decision was made early on that they would keep their dresses a surprise until the wedding day. They made two appointments an hour apart and drove down to BHLDN in Seattle together. Ashleigh and Bri-anne each had the same stylist working with them to ensure that they didn't choose the same dress.

Unknowingly at the time, they each walked out with a two-piece dress that day.

Pemberton's majestic mountains and quiet valleys are where they spent their first anniversary together, and it's the location they chose to marry too.

Knowing all too well that they would be quite restricted in the time that they could personally put towards planning their wedding day, Ashleigh & Bri-anne decided to hire a planner once they'd locked in the venue.

With an outdoor wedding comes the risk of it being interrupted by weather. The forecast wasn't looking great for the day, but they each crossed their fingers that the worst of it would hold off.

The morning of the wedding was relaxing. The brides had their hair and makeup done together with their friends, and when the time came to put their dresses on, they anxiously separated. It was in the field, with their bridal party watching from the balcony, that they had their first look. It's a special moment neither of them will ever forget.

The rain did hold off for the ceremony. In fact, there was really only a lightly sprinkle during dinner, which only meant that the newlyweds were gifted by mother nature with an incredible rainbow.

Warm and welcoming; that was the intended vibe of the wedding day and one that was delivered perfectly - a true reflection of the couple themselves. It was important for the lovers to not just celebrate their love for one another on the day, but also their love for everyone in their lives who have supported them over their years together.

An organic color palette was ideal, allowing the surrounding scenery to speak volumes. Big bouquets of natural greens and white florals, the styling had a real modern meets vintage vibe.

And, the incredible food by Collective Kitchen is something all the guests still rave about.

Under festoon lighting, that small group of just 40 celebrated a brand new chapter in Ashleigh and Bri-anne's life together.

Memorable, emotional and perfect.

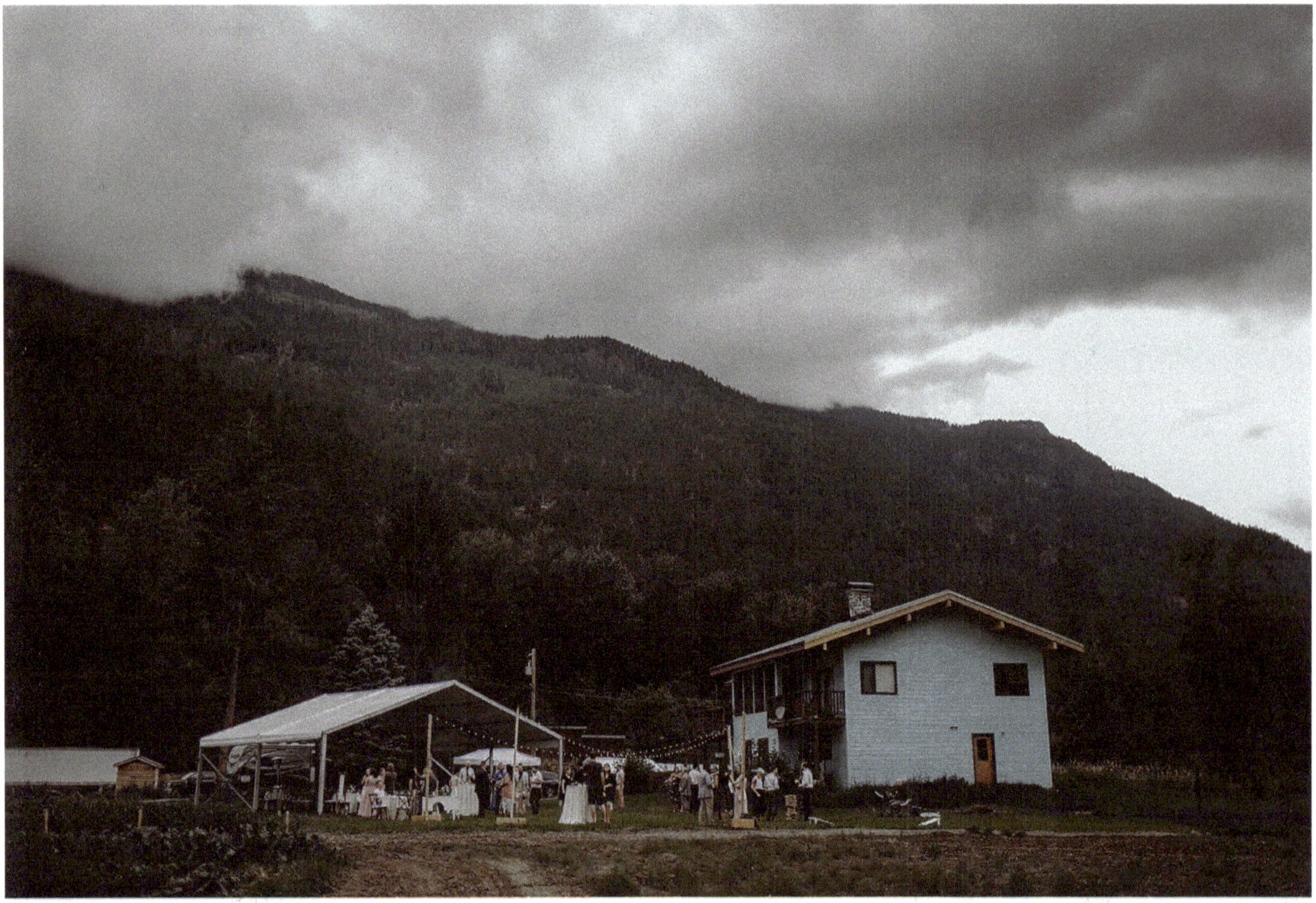

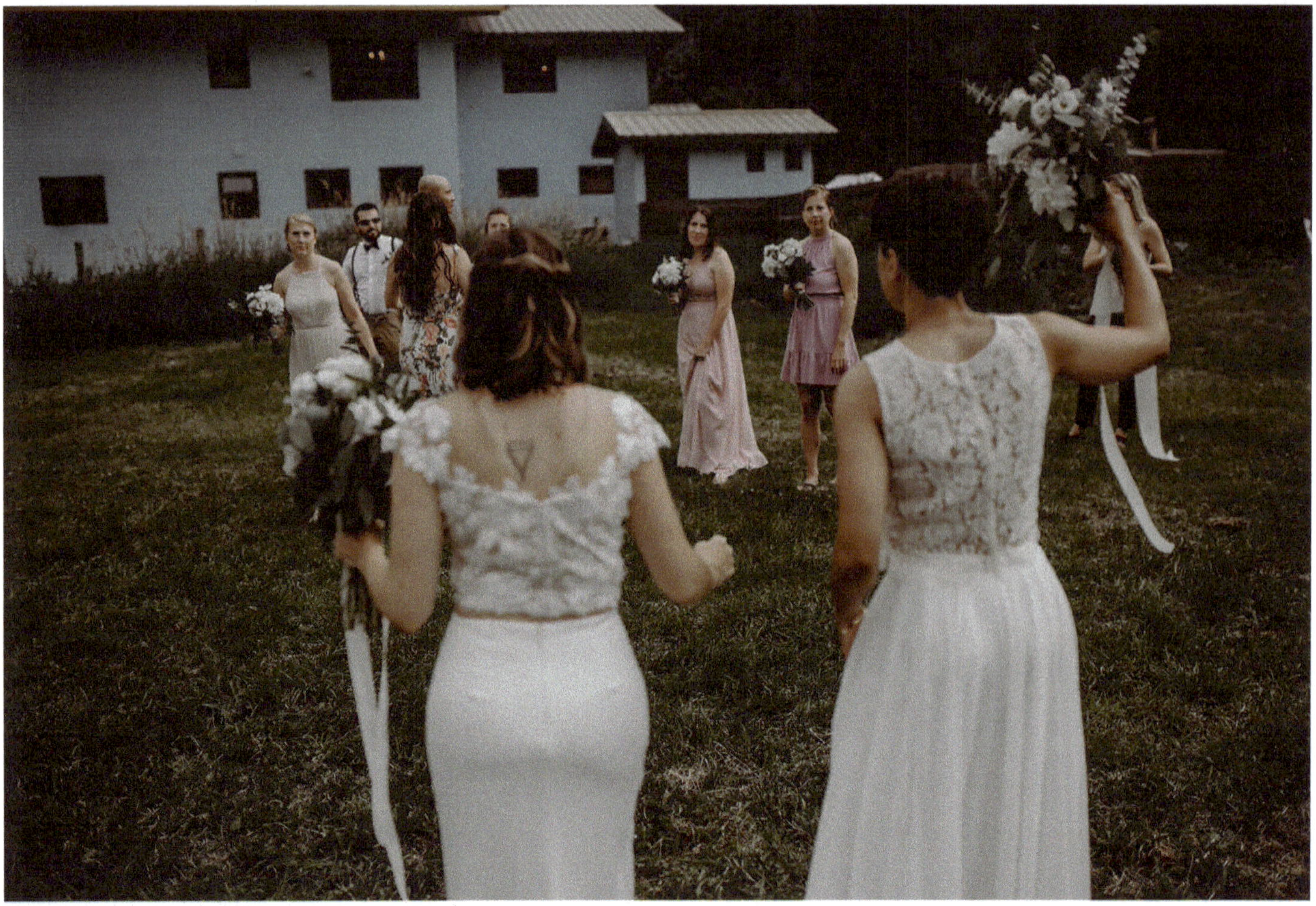

Bridal Boutique BHLDN | **Catering** Collective Kitchen | **Ceremony Venue** Blue House Organic Farm | **Celebrant** Friend | **Entertainment** Coast Mountain DJ's | **Event Planner & Stylist** Epic Events | **Florist** Billie's Flower House | **H&MU** Save the Date Beauty | **Hair Piece** Powder Blue Bijoux | **Photographer** Erin Fraser | **Prop Hire** The Little Wedding Shoppe | **Signage** Spring Meadow Co. | **Transport** VIP Whistler

Tovah,

When I first met you, I didn't know what was going to happen. But I knew that one way or another you were going to be someone special to me. I could have never guessed following my intuition would bring so much joy in my life.

Just like that, we fell in love. First slowly, then all at once. We now have this bond that is sacred and cherished and within it, we have built a home. In Letters to a Young Poet, Rainer Maria Rilke says "believe in a love that is being stored up for you like an inheritance, and have faith that in this love there is a strength and a blessing so large that you can travel as far as you wish without having to step outside of it." And Tov, we have that. I never thought it was something I would ever have or would ever deserve to have, but I feel your love with me everywhere I go. I feel it so strong within me that I could close my eyes and find you in the dark. I could be miles away from you and still find my way back to you. And together, I know we can navigate whatever unknowns life may bring us.

You are my calm in the storm. My twin soul. My whole heart. When I look at you, I see everything I have fallen in love with. Your passion for learning and connecting, your drive to make a difference, your fight for justice, and your loyalty for those you love. You have shown me the power of being completely vulnerable and surrendering to someone. You have shown me the beauty of living authentically.

Together, we make sense and make each other stronger. We push each other to become the best versions of ourselves. We cheer each other successes, cry together during the low times, and laugh at the ridiculous ones. We are each other's advocates and confidantes. I promise I will never take any of that for granted. There is no other lover I want to fall asleep next to. No other partner I want to build a future with. No other mother I want to co-parent with. No other friend I want to grow old with. You are it. And I promise to remind you every day that you are all those things to me and so much more. I love you, and will continue to love you, for the rest of my days in this lifetime and the next.

Tovah Rachel Blumenthal, Will you Marry me?

Charcuterie Board Savour & Graze | **Day of Planner** Peachy Keen Coordination, LLC | **Florist** Smallyard Flowers | **Location** Airbnb
Photographer The Documentarist | **Proposal Workshop [Speech Assistance]** Rooted & Wild PDX | **Rentals & Decor** Vintage Meets Modern Portland
Rings Elaine B. Jewelry | **Signage & Calligraphy** Letters & Dust | **Videographer** Forest & Ivory Films

THE REAL COST OF WEDDING JEWELS

with Emily Chelsea Jewelry, www.emilychelsea.com

They say diamonds are a girl's best friend, and when it comes to engagement rings and wedding jewelry, some people dream of having a diamond. However, at what cost?

We spoke with Emily, of Emily Chelsea Jewelry, to get the answers.

Tell us a little bit more about Emily Chelsea Jewelry.
I started Emily Chelsea Jewelry out of a small studio in Philadelphia before I graduated college. I got my BFA in jewelry, metals and CAD, so I had always hoped I could continue to grow my business and stay in the jewelry industry.

My first jewelry internship was a dream come true- it combined responsible sourcing and creating jewelry [that combo was unheard of at the time], and that was the first time I learned that it could be possible to combine two of my passions. I worked at a few jewelry stores from 2011 to 2015, gaining valuable knowledge about how to run a jewelry store- I'm so thankful for that time and all that I learned!

I went full time with my business in 2015 while living in California and then eventually settled down in Philadelphia, with my showroom in the same neighborhood where I started out in the first place.

How much does an engagement ring [or wedding ring] cost?
It really can depend! If you are getting a large center stone, that can really dominate the price of the ring, especially if that stone is a diamond. Sapphires are more affordable alternatives, and a popular diamond alternative is moissanite, which is a lab-grown gem that is super sparkly, super durable, but a fraction of the cost of a diamond.

I always price out the ring portion separately from a center stone, so something like a simple solitaire could be between US$600-$1200 [plus the center stone], and as you add more stones, the price increases.

Wedding or commitment bands are a little less complicated- the thinner rings without stones are around US$200-$500, and wider rings range from US$400-$900, depending on the width.

What are the different factors that go into pricing a ring?
Like I said, if you are getting a larger center stone, that almost always dominates the price. A classic round one-carat diamond that meets all of my criteria is around $7000, and the price can change so much based on the different qualities [carat, color, cut, clarity].

For those not looking for a diamond that large [or a diamond at all!] a great budget for an engagement ring is between $2000-$4000. You usually can get a beautiful and custom ring for that price.

We also know that cost doesn't just mean financial. Jewelry can have a huge environmental cost too. Why is working mindfully important to you?
It is so difficult for me to put this into a short answer as there are so many complex issues that compel me to work mindfully.

The short answer is; that because I care about this planet and the people and creatures on it.

I was raised on the values to love and care for everyone and everything. I've spent my life hiking and traveling, and I have such a passion for this earth and the natural beauty of it. It's no secret that humans have a huge impact on this earth and that it is our responsibility to take care of it.

I was also raised to have a heart of compassion for others. We all deserve the right and privilege of opportunity and good health, but unfortunately, that is not everyone's reality. If I am not working to change that through my everyday work, then I'm not taking advantage of the opportunity offered to me.

When we imagine mining, metals and gems, we imagine huge holes in the ground and large scale environmental damage. Is that what it's really like?
On the one hand, yes, it is like that. There are several large mines that are

so large you can see them from outer space.

There are also much smaller mines that can be done underground that you get to through long vertical tunnels. They may not appear as large, but they certainly can have large repercussions. Because these types of mines are smaller, they can be a lot less regulated in terms of safety, environmental degradation, poor labor practices, etc.

And, there are also hobby fossickers who spend a weekend every now and again searching for stones. Sometimes beautiful gems can be found right on the surface.

We've heard of the Kimberly Process when buying diamonds, does it mean that the diamonds are conflict-free?
When we hear the term "conflict free" we think it means "free of conflict." Unfortunately, that is not what it means in the case of diamonds.

When the Kimberley Process Certification Scheme was passed, it was in response to the sale of "rough diamonds used by rebel movements or their allies to finance armed conflicts aimed at undermining legitimate governments'." This is a very narrow definition and does not include other types of conflict, including but not limited to, corrupt practices, human rights abuses, and environmental degradation.

The KP also does not weigh in on other areas of diamond production, such as cutting and polishing, which can include worker safety issues, pay inequity, and child and indentured labor.

Currently, I do not work with any newly mined diamonds, only recycled or repurposed stones. There are a few initiatives in place that are working to source diamonds more responsibly, such as Diamonds for Peace and the Diamond Development Initiative. However, they are still in the early stages, and I am unaware of a reliable and consistent source through either organization.

I strongly encourage customers to not stop at "conflict free" as their checkmark for "responsibly sourced." The more consumers demand something better, the more the industry is forced to change- for the better.

What does it really mean when you say that the metals and gems that you use are ethically sourced?
Sourcing ethically means to source without doing harm to the environment, humans and animals.

I do this by either using recycled or Fairmined gold and by using repurposed or traceable [back to a responsible source] gemstones.

Buying recycled is great because it is zero impact. When you buy Fairmined gold or newly mined stones from a responsible source, you are contributing positively to the current market. All of the newly mined stones I work with come from either Montana, Australia, or Sri Lanka, and I just started working with stones from a brand new organization called Moyo Gems.

Moyo Gems work with the female miners of Tanzania and work to empower female miners to mine safely, work better and improve financial stability.

Fairmined gold is an amazing initiative that sources gold from third party verified mines. Fairmined ensures that the gold is coming from legitimately organized mines that have fair labor practices, safe conditions, fair pay, and include environmental restoration. All things that are so important to me.

Although sometimes the price tag for jewelry made by artisan jewelers like myself is a little higher than what you would find in your local shopping mall, you'll have more control over choosing a ring that has a lower social and environmental impact.

You can find Emily Chelsea's beautiful collection of ready-made engagement and wedding jewelry, as well as custom-designed jewels, here: www.emilychelsea.com

CELESTE & ERICA
PHOTOGRAPHY BY CALDER PHOTOGRAPHY
www.calderphoto.com

IDAHO, USA

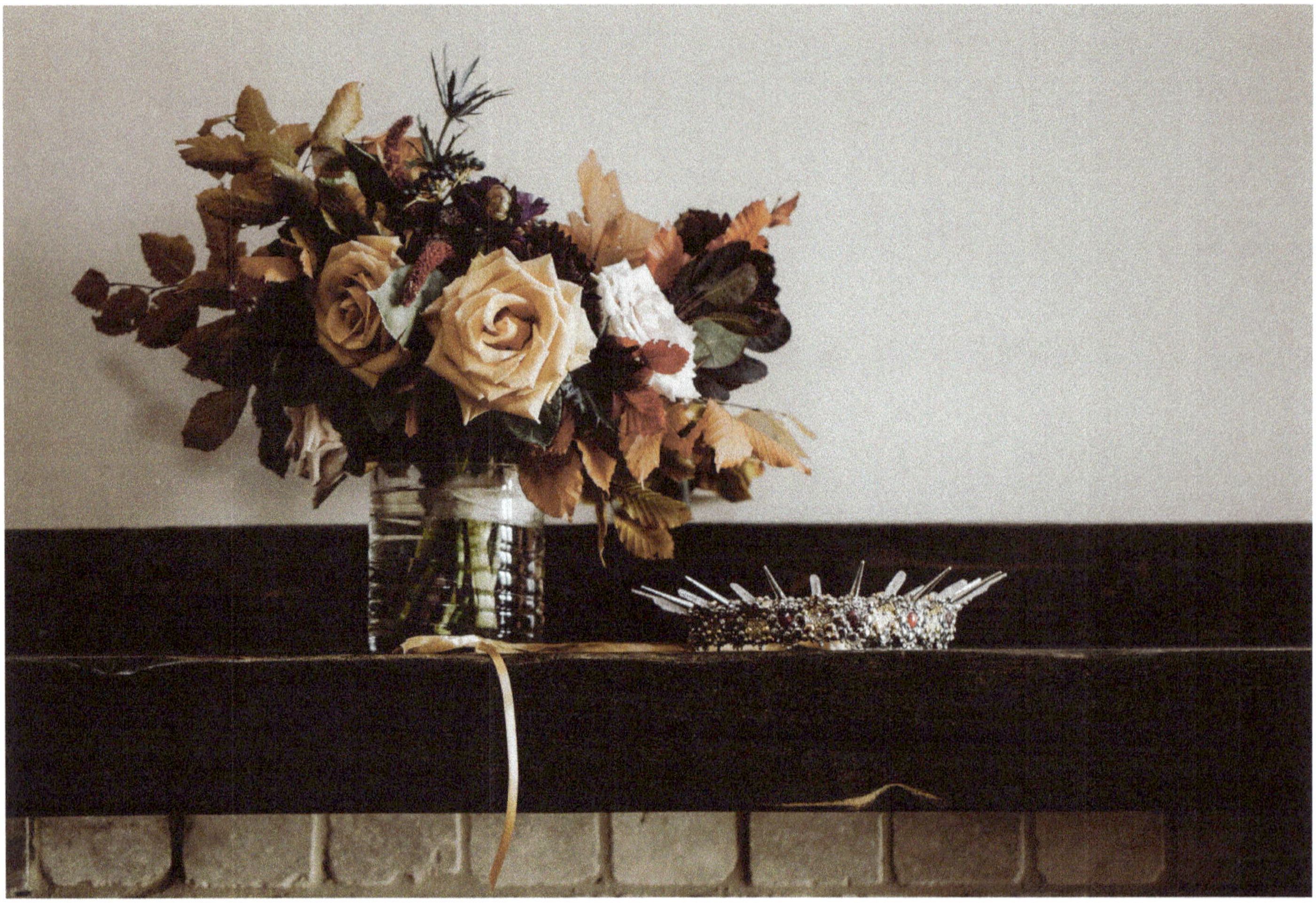
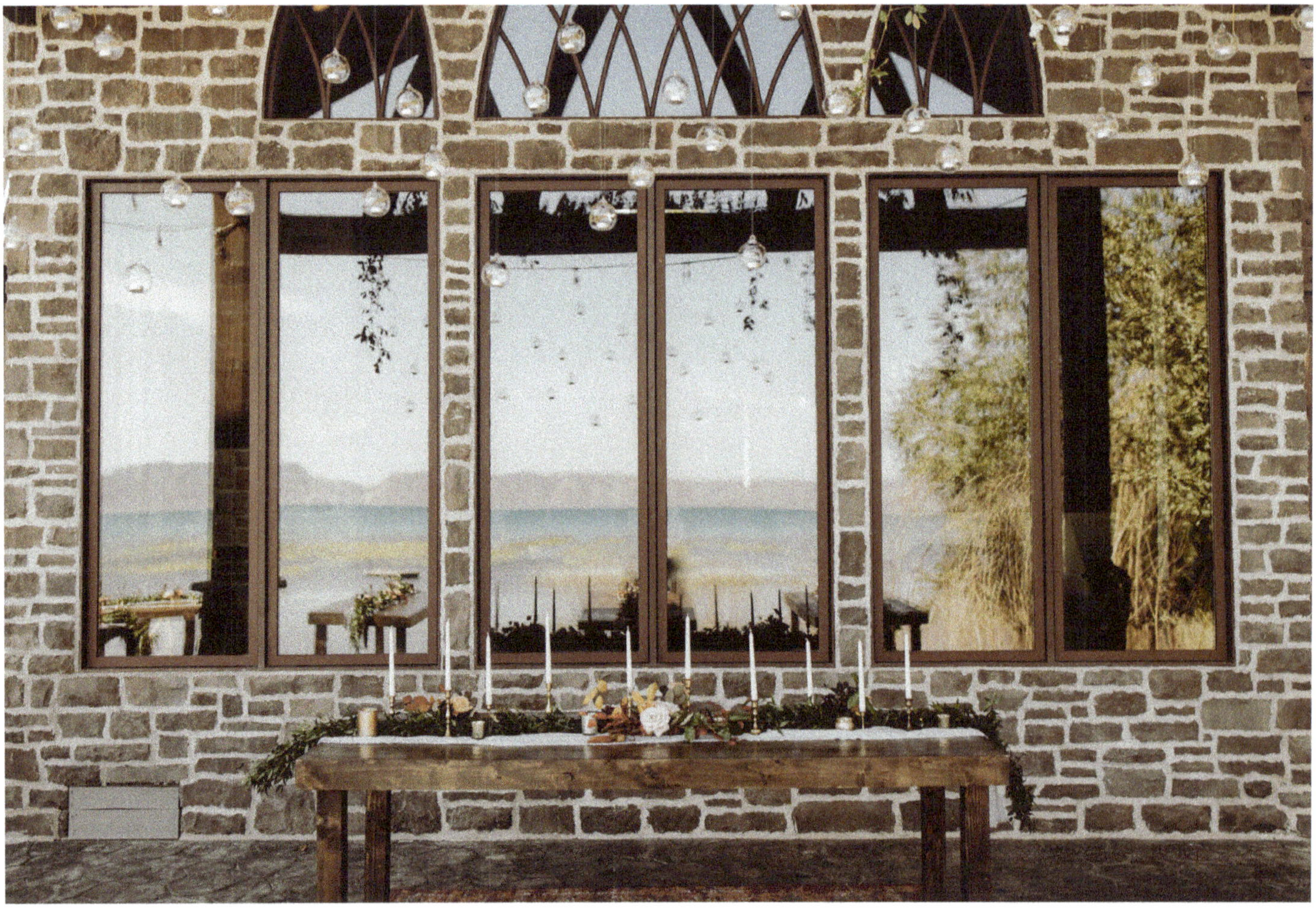

When Erica and Celeste first met, it was through exes. It wasn't ideal at the time, but after working through how they were both feeling, they knew that everything was meant to happen for a reason. They've been virtually inseparable ever since.

Celeste spent time in Hawaii after high school and at a liberal arts school formed some of her most important relationships, particularly with Isaac and Sheyna, her two best friends. Erica knew that she couldn't propose without their help.

Erica planned a trip to Hawaii, inviting their best friends from Utah to come along as well. Isaac, who is a musician, had a gig on one of the nights they were visiting- the perfect cover. He invited the lovers and their friends to the gig and at a certain point in his set, started playing Celeste and Erica's 'song'. About halfway through the song, he paused, and Erica stood up and got down on one knee. She'd also arranged for Celeste's family to be on Facetime so that they were truly surrounded by the people most special to them.

Although these lovers have been together for nine years, they spent just three months planning their perfect wedding day.

They chose Bear Lake as the destination. It was the place where Erica and Celeste had taken their very fist getaway as a young couple, and it's been a place that they've always been drawn towards. They've found themselves back there multiple times during their relationship to recharge, to grieve and to get back in tune with one another when things get a little tough.

For Celeste, finding something to wear was always going to be stress-free - she had just planned to find something simple online. However, her younger sister was determined for her to have a bridal shop experience and swiftly booked an appointment. It was a blessing in disguise, and even she was surprised at how many gowns she fell in love with and felt beautiful in.

Erica wanted to feel beautiful, comfortable and herself, and together the couple decided that a t-shirt and suit, accessorized with some custom jewelry, was entirely her.

Most of the decor was done by the couple, with help from their loved ones, in the lead up to the big day. Celeste's oldest brother built their triangle wedding arch from locally sourced wood, and the rugs, candlesticks, glass globes and lighting were all collected along the wedding planning journey. They even had their best friends marry them.

They did away with any pressures of expectations for the day and stuck true to who they are as a couple. Their day was entirely centered around their love story and everything they wanted the day to celebrate. Every detail was intentional.

Erica and Celeste walked down the aisle to Amel Larrieux's 'Make Me Whole,' sung by Celeste's best friend. And although during vows, it was hard for both the lovers to keep their emotions together, it was those moments that they will never forget.

And, in an impeccably styled cabin in Bear Lake Idaho, with 75 of their most-loved people, they celebrated. They celebrated their love and their commitment to always walk through life together side by side, never giving up on the other.

Accessories Child of Wild, Vitaly | **Cake** Flour and Flourish | **Catering** Marlene Noda | **Ceremony & Reception Venue** Cabin at Bear Lake Idaho **Celebrant** Steve Loso | **Crystal Crown** Amaroq | **Decorative Elements** Magnolia Flower Co | **Entertainment** Poetik C | **Engagement Rings** Todd Reed Design | **Florist** Magnolia Flower Co | **Gown Designer** Leanne Marshall | **H&MU** Victoria Hewlett | **Photographer** Calder Photography **Prop & Furniture Hire** Alpine Event Co | **Stationery** Steve Loso | **Suit Designer** Calvin Klein | **Wedding Rings** Todd Reed Design, Shubachs Jewelers

MARRIED TO A MAN & IN LOVE WITH A WOMAN
Words by Kayla

It was September of 2016- fall term had just started, and my last class on Monday was Leadership. This was a class that was required of any member of the Associated Student Government, which I was a part of.

Typically, this class was only filled with said ASG members, but in this particular term, that was not the case. I walked into that new classroom, recognizing my peers that I got to work with when my eyes shifted to the only seat available, which was next to someone with slicked-back hair and sporty clothes on. When she turned around to look at me as I approached the seat, I felt my heart drop right onto the floor, and time stop.

Convinced that everyone heard and saw it fall, I quickly shuffled to my seat beside her. The first thing that got me was that big, bright smile; next were her amber eyes, resembling those of a lioness.

I always felt at ease and safe near her. We bantered back and forth, ooh-ing and aah-ing at how many crazy things we had in common until the class had to interrupt us and begin. That was only the beginning.

I can't pinpoint a date when I knew that my feeling for Megan were more, though I wish I could. I do remember noticing how much I would miss her when we were apart, how I wanted to be near her all of the time, and how my heart felt when she'd message me or smile at me.

Whenever something went wrong, she was who I wanted to turn to first, and when I had something to celebrate, I wanted to celebrate it beside her. When I would think about my future, she was who I spent it with, and all of the love songs became about her.

We became close almost instantaneously and would create any excuse we could just to be in the company of the other person. I was in denial of my feelings for a while because I had a hard time believing that Megan could possibly have feelings for me, but also I was in denial because of how I grew up and the complexity of the situation [me freshly being in a straight-passing relationship with a man]. I was in foster care from about 11 to 18, and the home I was in for the majority of that time was very religious, and many homophobic comments were made. I was struggling back then with my sexuality, but had to hide it and ignore it.

When rumors at my school spread that I was bisexual, and my guardians found out, they were furious and asked me if it was true; I had to lie to survive and avoid punishment. From then on, my sexuality would try to surface, and I'd stuff it deeper and deeper away; afraid of facing the truth. So when I began to fall for Megan (and HARD), my mind was at war with itself. On the one hand, this woman was everything I could ever hope for and want in a partner, and then on the other, I was absolutely terrified of coming out, and the thought of who I would lose in the process was scary to fathom.

On Christmas of 2016, Megan sent me a poem she wrote about me, and admitted her feelings for me, and my stomach was in knots. I was flattered, excited, surprised, and scared. A few days later, we met at our usual café hang spot, and talked about it all. I admitted my feelings for her, but that I didn't think I was ready to be out, and felt conflicted because I also felt guilty about having these feelings while in a relationship.

Megan was flattered, excited, surprised, and sad. She, rightfully so, didn't want to be the secret, and so we were stuck. We wanted so badly to be together, but it just felt so close but so out of reach.

After Megan and I had our deep conversation about us and our feelings, I gave it a lot of thought and was just about ready to break it off with the guy I was dating, when another wrench got thrown into it all: I found out I was pregnant. I had always wanted to be a mom, so I thought maybe this was some sort of sign that this was what I was supposed to do, what my life was supposed to look like.

Megan was devastated when I told her, because she wanted that to be her that I was having a child with. Once I told my boyfriend, and then his family, they were like, "well, you guys gotta get married!" and so we started planning.

I was thrilled to be pregnant and so excited to be a mom; it was something I dreamt about since I was little. During this time, I felt so confused. I was partially blinded by the excitement of a baby and a wedding, but also still wanting Megan around all the time. She began to slowly pull away, because it became too hard for her, which I understood and felt awful for. We would still hang out for hours on end, multiple times a week, and I still loved every moment we got to be together.

When we were apart, we were constantly texting one another. We would say that, above all, we cared deeply for one another and wanted to at least remain friends; we hated the thought of losing one another. But, I knew the end was coming.

And in June, after I got married, it did.

Megan stopped answering my messages, and we stopped hanging out, and just like that, we were strangers.

And then, my then-husband and I began having marital problems.

We tried several books, talking to others, to each other, and nothing seemed to fix it. I stopped caring, and I did not feel wanted. In the end, we were just not meant to be.

I don't usually dream or remember my dreams, but I dreamt about Megan during this time. Everything reminded me of her, and I was so sad, and felt guilty for feeling all of these feelings again, while being married. I cried a lot, I would get angry, but that did not last long because I just missed her.

And then we slowly started talking again, and eventually hung out. By hangout #2, it was like no time had stopped. All of those feelings, memories, and everything flooded back, but in a more intense way.

We talked again about what had happened between us in the past and admitted that we never really stopped loving one another. I eventually ended up coming out to my now-ex-husband and his family, moved out, and started my own life; this time, with Megan in it.

In the beginning, when I was going through the divorce and custody agreement, I was kind of a wreck, and I was super thankful for Megan in those times because I lost a lot of people in this whole process, and having her as a constant was super comforting. Since moving in together, and being able to be us, and together, I have felt so free and at peace. I am the happiest I have ever been, I feel safest in her arms, and she is who I want to wake up next to for the rest of my life, who I want to drink coffee with at 7:00 at night, to laugh with, and conquer the world beside.

When she asked me to marry her, I felt like I needed to be pinched, because all I ever wanted was to marry her, spent our lives together, and create our own legacy to pass down to our kids. And it is all happening before my eyes, it's like a movie or book, and I still can't sometimes believe, that this is my life. I am so blessed.

Megan says she was confused back then because she couldn't understand why it had to happen the way it did; us loving each other but not being able to be together. We were [and are!] perfect for each other, but it felt like the world was against us for whatever reason. But, since being together now, it makes sense why it had to happen the way it did.

We both learned a lot in the time apart, and it made us stronger for one another. She says she's the happiest she's ever been, has never laughed so much in her life, and can't wait for us to spend our lives together.

EMILY & LIZ

PHOTOGRAPHY BY THE NOOK
www.insidethenook.com

MELBOURNE, AUSTRALIA

On a sunrise hike up the headland of Noosa, through a whole bundle of nerves, Liz blurted out 'will you marry me?'. Emily's response, 'of course I'll marry you!'.

They spent the next twelve months planning their wedding day.

Emily and Liz set their visions on a low-key, high-fun wedding - more of a love celebration meets dance party meets cheese-eating shindig. Because brunching together has become a Saturday morning ritual, they chose one of their favorite Melbourne spots, Little Henri, to host the affair.

Emily loves to DIY, although much to Liz's annoyance, hates finishing projects. Wedding DIY projects went to much the same effect. Immediately after deciding on a color scheme of their favorite colors, yellow and pink, Emily decided it would be a fantastic excuse to make hundreds of pom-poms. Several iterations of what they would actually be used for came and went, but ultimately they realized that there just wasn't the space for them. The savvy brides turned them into a ridiculous collar and lead for their adopted greyhound, Toast.

It turns out that DIY weddings aren't for everyone.

Wedding days are often imperfectly perfect, and that's precisely Emily & Liz's experience. They had it all; rain-soaked muddy gowns, panicked phone calls between bridesmaids about logistical errors, their dog nearly running onto a road, a tear in the bodice of Liz's dress, both brides tripping up the stairs in the aisle, vendors mixing up their names, a case of a disappearing cake, and drunken guests getting inappropriate. You really couldn't make up some of the stuff that the newlyweds encountered.

Their biggest mistake was relying on Uber to get from the first look location to the venue. Six bridesmaids and two brides in full gowns standing in mud on the side of the road was far too stressful- looking back, they wish they'd hired a couple of cars.

But, for Emily and Liz, something magical was felt when they looked into their lover's face, moments after placing a ring on her finger with the blurred faces of everyone they love cheering in the background. The mistakes just didn't, and don't, matter because love won.

There were plenty of moments that will never be forgotten. Like during the ceremony where their celebrant, Precious, had organized a sweet surprise. Emily and Liz had let it slip to Precious that they were huge rom-com fans, and so Precious arranged for the couple to have their very own rom-com moment. A list of 23 things Emily loved about Liz was randomly distributed amongst the crowd and readout, one by one, by all their favorite people.

The speeches by their maids of honor were also phenomenal; every guest was taken on a rollercoaster of tears, laughter, and joyfulness.

And, the first dance, where it felt like they were the only two people in the room, but they were, in fact, surrounded by their loved ones singing Taylor Swift's 'Lover.'

Then, their band, White Tree Band, totally brought the party vibe- a vendor that they were so desperate to make work for the day. The dancefloor was full well into the night.

Although being married might be a boring, government-sanctioned legally-binding agreement, Emily and Liz are honored and thrilled to have it. To have their love, friendship, and family recognized in the eyes of the law is a privilege she won't ever forget, and they thank all the LGBTQIA+ folks before them who paved the way for their particular union.

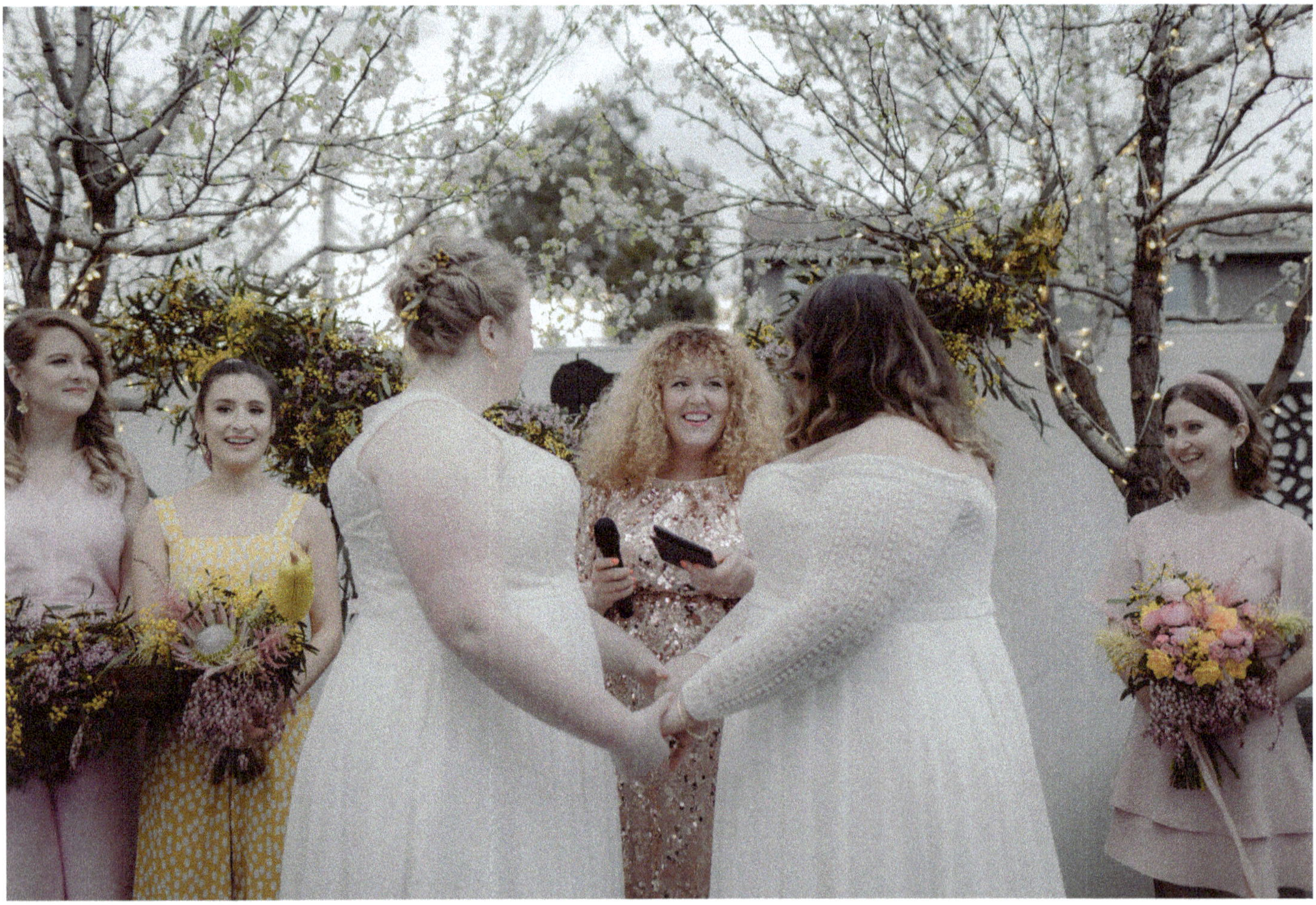

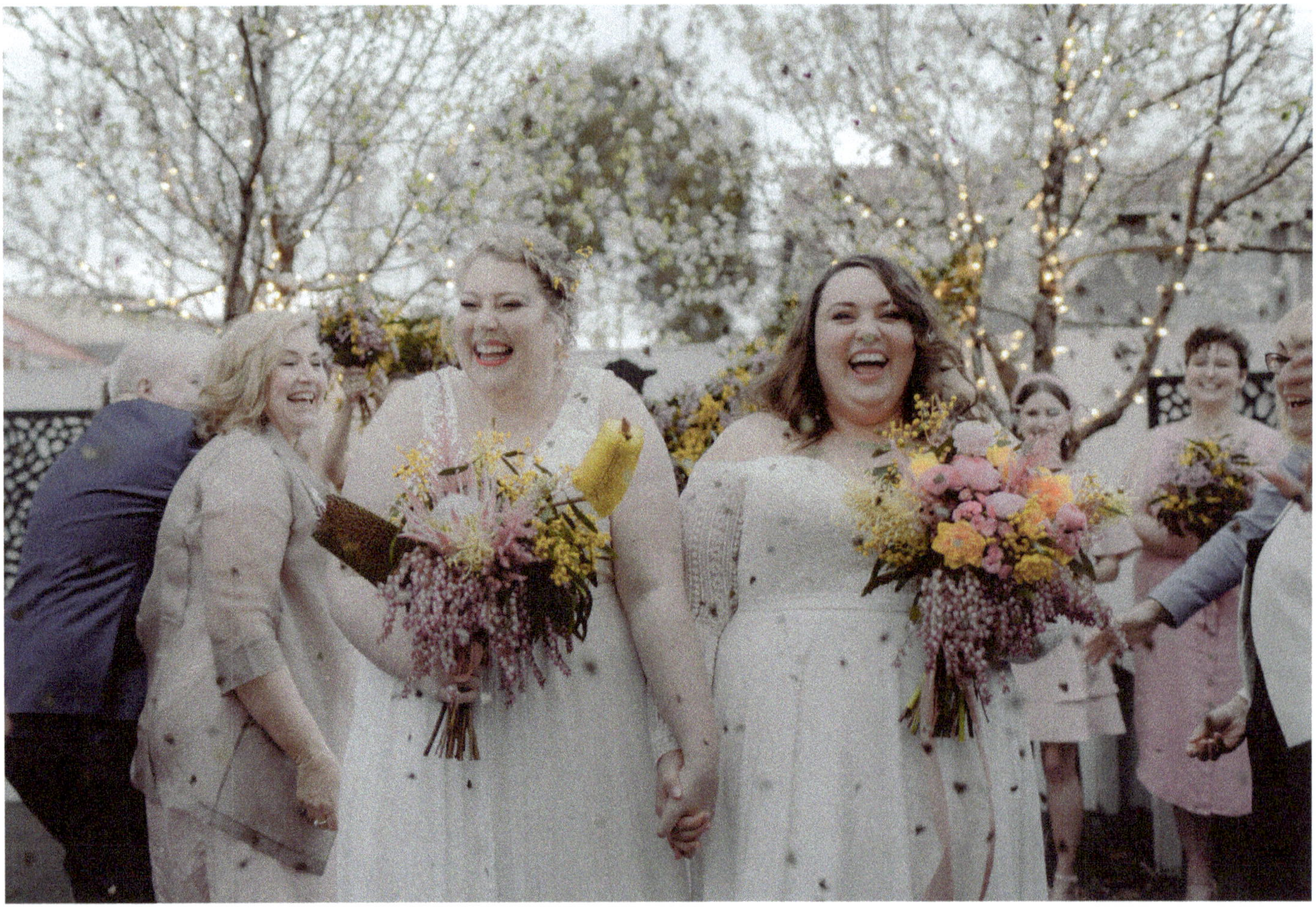

Accessories Connie And Luna | **Bridal Boutique** Designer Bridal House | **Cake** Cherry Cakes | **Catering** Little Henri | **Ceremony & Reception Venue** Little Henri | **Celebrant** Precious Celebrations | **Entertainment** White Tree Band | **Engagement Rings** Windfall Jewellery | **Florist** Good Grace & Humour | **Gown Designer** Studio Levana | **H&MU** Elle Cosgriff Hair, Madz Artistry, Made You Blush, Johnny Thorpe | **Photographer** The Nook | **Prop & Furniture Hire** Always Eventive | **Shoes** Bared | **Stationery** Hannah Kallady, MOO Print | **Transport** Uber | **Wedding Rings** The Line of Sun

THE RISE OF MICRO WEDDINGS

Words by Fairina Cheng, of Fairina Cheng Jewellery
www.fairinachengjewellery.com

Epic white weddings with hundreds of guests and a six-figure budget are making way for the "micro wedding" trend. The micro wedding, typified by single-digit guest lists and intimate ceremonies, are fast becoming the celebration du jour for couples valuing authenticity over grandeur.

I mean, how romantic is the thought of having just a tiny handful of wedding guests, people who you are most close to, your biggest love cheerleaders, there with you when you tie the knot?

As a custom jeweler who some may describe as a bit unconventional, I am working with more and more couples who either elope or get married with just their family and close friends in attendance. They want their wedding to be about them, and don't care for flashy affairs and blingy engagement rings. Instead, they want their special day to be authentic, meaningful, and full of fun memories.

Generally, couples opt for a micro wedding because they're keen to have a stress-free, drama-free event where they can enjoy themselves and the company of their favorite people.

As a bonus, micro weddings usually cost less, which means couples can focus on personalized details like unusual venues and handcrafted wedding and engagement rings.

It also means that fewer couples are heading into marriage in debt, something that you will be super thankful that you did later on down the track.

However, to pull off an epic mico-wedding of your own, there are a few things to keep in mind.

Keep the guest list small
Start with the five most important people in your lives. If that doesn't cover it, allow five more. Don't just include people because they would be upset if they weren't invited; instead, ask yourself, 'would I be sad if they weren't there?' It's easy to add one person to the list and then feel guilty about not inviting the ten other people in that social circle, so be selective. Remember that no one else, not your family or your friends, can dictate who you want there on the big day. Hold strong to that one. Weddings are notorious for bringing out [well-intentioned, I'm sure] opinions of others.

Get creative with your venue
With fewer people, it's easier to be flexible with your location. Go beyond the traditional wedding venues and think about your favorite restaurants, bars and places that mean something to you as a couple. This could be the park where you had your first kiss or the place where you had your first date. Sometimes the most untraditional places are where you'll get the best photos.

Having fewer people to cater for may also mean that you can have the destination wedding you've been dreaming of! Take your favorite people with you and have the kind of wedding you would never have been able to with a hundred guests in tow.

Put your money where your heart is
With couples spending an average of more than $30k on their weddings, micro weddings empower couples to spend their cash on the things that matter most to them. For you, this might mean great photographs that capture memories you'll back on years down the track, or a bespoke ring that is completely customized to you and your partner's shared history.

As a jeweler, the most interesting rings are those that feature hidden symbols that lovers can keep secret or choose to share. I love subtle references to the place you met, memories you hold dear, or quirky symbols that mean the world to you both. There's nothing quite like a personalized piece of story-telling jewellery you can carry with you every day of your married life.

ALYSHA & MICHAELA

PHOTOGRAPHY BY FOX & KIN
www.foxandkin.com

SYDNEY, AUSTRALIA

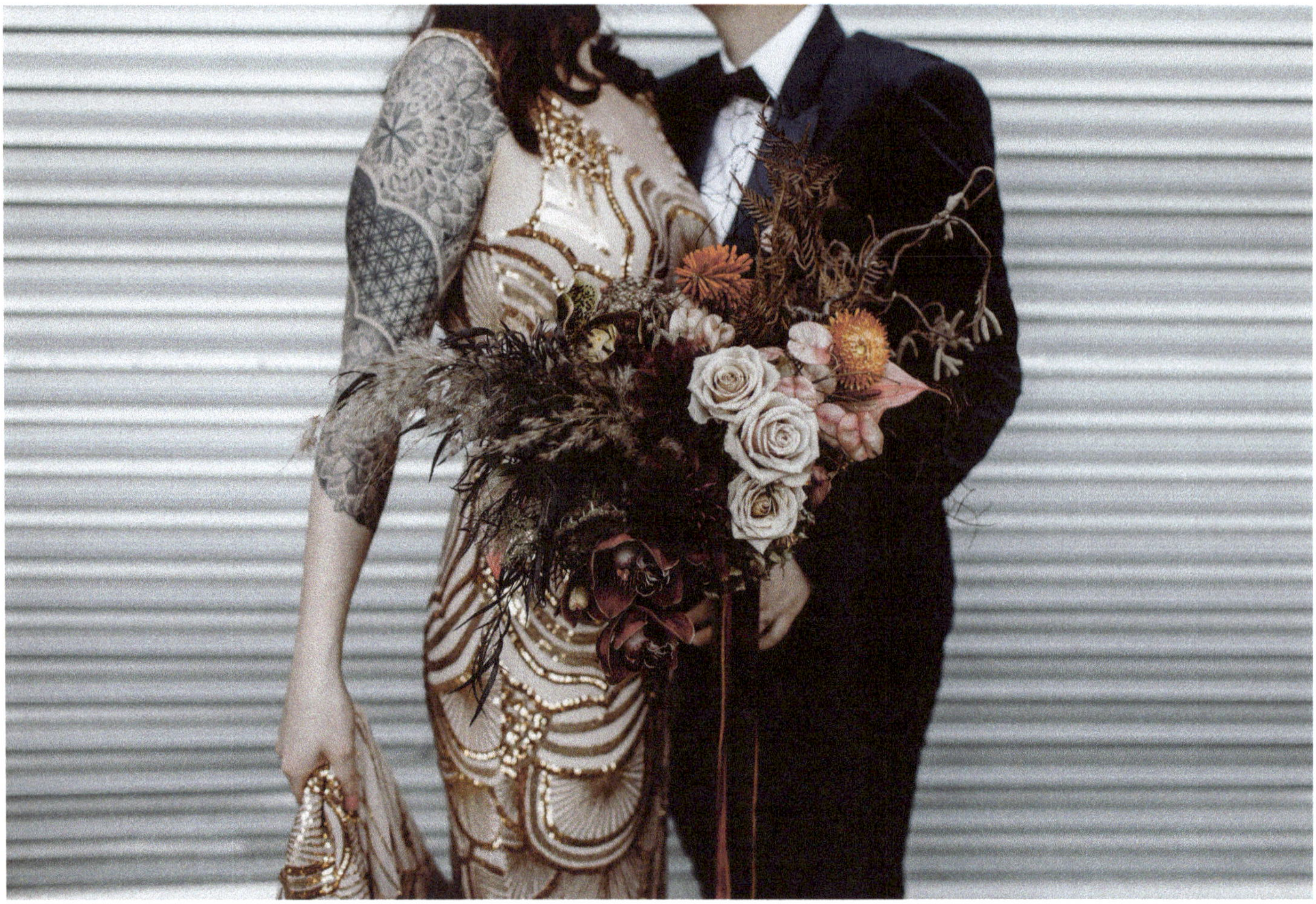

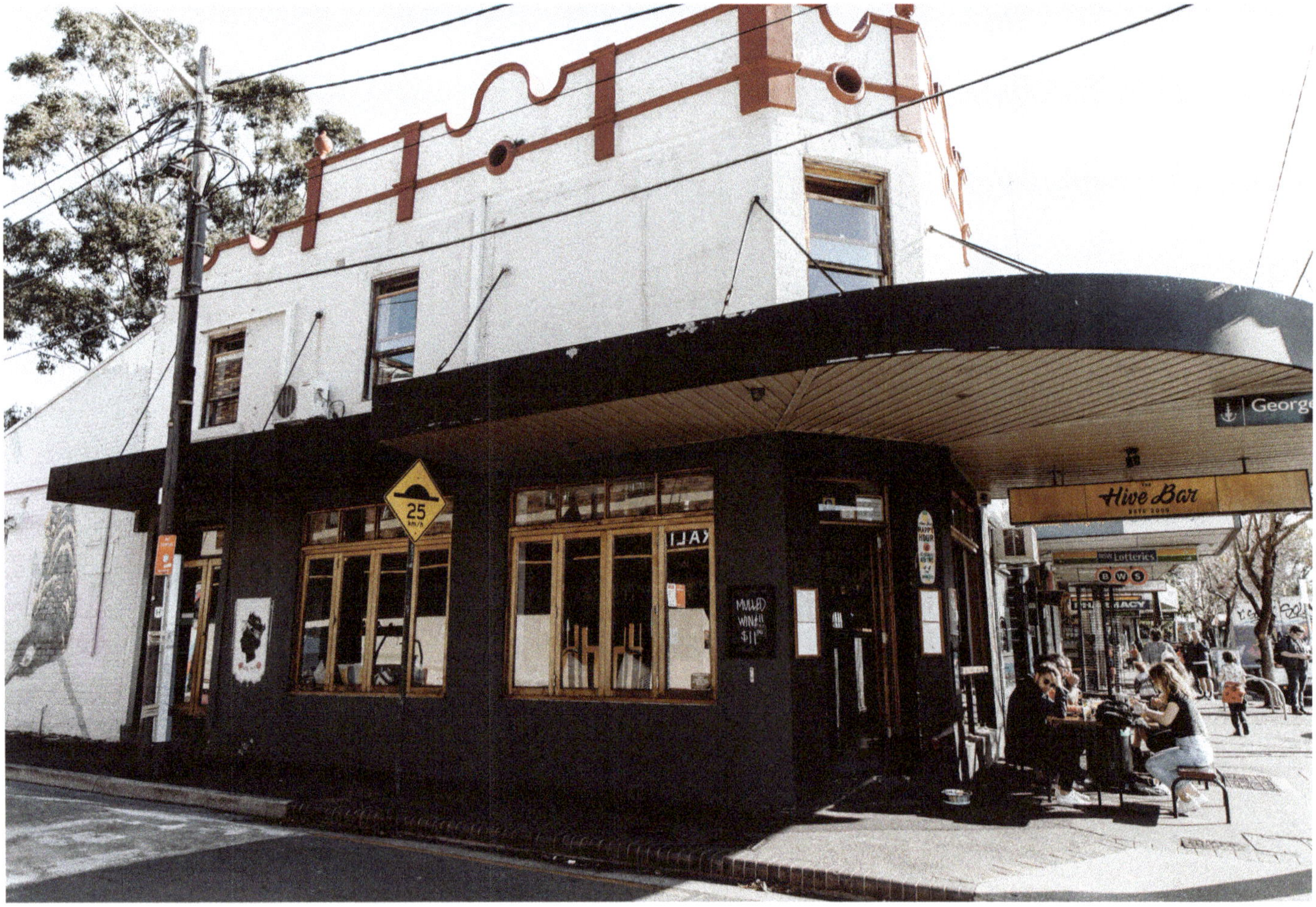

25
MULLED WINE!! $11
Hive Bar
Lotteries
BWS

It wasn't a secret that Mic was going to propose to Alysha, soon. In fact, Alysha helped with details of the ring, but the final design wasn't revealed until the jeweler shared an image of the ring on Instagram- before Mic had a chance to give it to Alysha. There were big plans for a proposal, but right there on the couch while they were watching TV together seemed like the perfect moment.

Wedding planning was sometimes stressful; it isn't easy to plan a wedding in just eight months. For Alysha and Mic, a wedding day that represented them, nothing formal but also nothing boring, was most important. A full vegan menu was also important, and Three Blue Ducks went above and beyond, most guests had no idea that everything [including the cake!] was vegan-friendly. The industrial look and vibe of the venue was perfect for their evening affair.

For Mic, finding an outfit was easy; she found a velvet jacket online for the first outfit and had a custom suit created by Shane Ave. However, Alysha dreamed of a long sleeve velvet jumpsuit to wear under a tulle skirt she'd fallen in love with and lined up a designer to make it happen. That designer left it all to the last minute, and unfortunately, it just wasn't the jumpsuit that Alysha envisioned. Two weeks before the wedding day she found herself frantically trying to find something that matched the color of the skirt and found a top online - four days before the wedding.

Thankfully, the drama of wedding outfits didn't follow through to the wedding day [apart from a frantic loop back to grab a bra and a 30-minute delay in the ceremony to get said bra].

Alysha and Mic's sisters, who were bridesmaids on the day, gathered together in the hotel for the morning. It was the relaxed start to the day the couple had hoped for.

Instead of heading straight into the ceremony, the lovers decided that they'd spend time together before the ceremony, calm their nerves, and have portraits photographed. It was a much-needed dose of quality time before the shenanigans of the wedding. It was also an excuse for two different outfits; one for before the ceremony, and another for the ceremony and reception.

After spending time together having portraits with their photographer, Fox & Kin, the bridesmaids and the couple head across to Hive Bar, the very same place the nearly-weds had their first date back in 2017. With celebratory margaritas in hand, it was an opportunity to take a moment and reflect before the hysteria of the evening began.

They each changed into their ceremony outfits, which were kept a surprise by some cheeky but clever bridesmaids. Mic wore a suit, and tulle skirt and top for Alysha. They all then head to the venue, Three Blue Ducks, where just over 100 of their family and friends where waiting to witness the lovers speak their vows and make their relationship legally a marriage.

After a vegan feast, but before things got too rowdy on the dancefloor, the couple were led to a now-empty ceremony area by their photographer. Taking time to cuddle together under the festoon lighting and stars as newly pronounced wife and wife, is one of the newlyweds' favorite moments to look back on.

And, although marriage hasn't really changed anything for Alysha and Mic, it has solidified their commitment. Their commitment to never give up on one another, to always be each other's best friend, and lover. Their commitment to always protect each other when they're most vulnerable, hands held walking through life together.

Bridal Boutique Penrith Bridal Center | **Bow Tie** YD | **Cake & Topper** Loretta's Vegan Cake | **Cufflinks** OTAA | **Desserts** Black Star Pastry | **Catering** Three Blue Ducks | **Ceremony & Reception Venue** Three Blue Ducks | **Celebrant** Marry Me Jacqueline Majer | **Decorative Elements** Three Blue Ducks | **Event Planner & Stylist** Alysha Roby | **Engagement & Wedding Rings** Heidi Gibson, Ainsleys Fine Jewellery | **Florist** Biophilia Blooms | **Flower Girl Outfits** Blue Sky Kids Land | **Gown Designers** Watters WTOO, Meshki, A&N Luxe | **Jacket** ASOS | **Lighting & Sound Hire** DJ Warehouse | **Photographer** Fox & Kin **Photo Booth** In The Booth | **Shoes** ASOS, Connor | **Stationery** Paperlust | **Suit Designer** Shane Ave | **Tattoo** Rusty Gee

PLANNING A MARRIAGE
...not just a wedding day

The wedding day is just that, a day. What comes after that is a new chapter in your relationship together, as a married couple.

It is so easy, incredibly easy, to get caught up in wedding planning. It's fun, exciting, and the prospect of having all your favorite people in the one room to celebrate your wedding is often a once in a lifetime opportunity.

But, being a married couple often comes with a few more complexities.

Bank accounts might merge, and significant financial decisions become joint decisions. Depending on where you're from, savings and debts you each had before the union also combine. There are changes to health care insurances, tax benefits...the list goes on.

Doing life together, legally married, means that there will be good and bad times. Boundaries will need to be set, and together, you'll need to figure out how to grow as individuals alongside one another.

So, while you're caught up figuring out which family member to invite or which color of napkin you'd love to grace on every plate, it can be easy to forget that what you're really planning is more than just a wedding day.

The wedding day is more of a 'beginning your marriage' party - so to speak. Overall, you're planning a marriage and making a vow to the future together.

A long, healthy, and [hopefully] successful marriage together.

It's essential in the wedding planning process that you sit down together to talk about how the legalities of marriage will change your relationship. Ask each other how you're feeling about it all, and if things are overwhelming, it might be beneficial to see a therapist, together or solo, to discuss the concerns.

You want to set yourselves up for the very best start to a marriage possible. Talk about what a successful marriage looks like, talk openly about your expectations within a marriage, and where you see yourself in five, ten, twenty years.

When you're planning the celebrations, try not to get carried away. It should be a day that is memorable, memorable in a way that is authentic to you and your partner.

Planning weddings are hard, but on the flip side, they can be excellent tools for learning how to communicate together better, budget appropriately, listen, compromise and make joint decisions- all skills that will be important in a marriage.

Take the pressure off yourselves to make it the best day of your lives. You're planning for the future, and there will absolutely be days that are just as incredible in your journey through life together.

And those people that you have meticulously invited to your now 'beginning your marriage' party, they're the people that you will likely lean on when things get tough and celebrate with when things are incredible. They're your community, your biggest love champions.

The most important thing to remember when wedding planning is if you're planning for a phenomenal marriage, there is no doubt that you'll have a phenomenal wedding day.

ANNE & KIRA

PHOTOGRAPHY BY LIGHTSMITH IMAGES
www.lightsmithimages.com.au

BRISBANE, AUSTRALIA

Kira had all good intentions when it came to making the day she proposed one of the most romantic of their lives. They had planned a trip to Queenstown, New Zealand, together for Kira's birthday and rented a picture-perfect cottage with a fireplace and incredible views of Lake Wakatipu and the surrounding mountains. There was even a helicopter ride planned.

Kira had planned a speech; it was about a page long. However, it was only during the second paragraph, just when she happened to mention their dog, Lyla, and how much they loved their pup, that she burst into sobs. She couldn't contain the emotions. Anne began to laugh at the timing of the sobs, and consequently distracted herself from what was actually happening at the moment. Kira presented a ring but had to ask the question again so that Anne could contain herself. It was imperfect, but so them.

They began planning a smaller wedding, 40 guests maximum. There were ideals of holding the wedding in a nice lodge, somewhere picturesque, somewhere that would require travel and overnight stay, but their family didn't take to the idea. They compromised and extended their guest list to 62. It did mean that Anne and Kira now had to consider something different from what they had initially hoped for. They found The Gardens Club right in the center of Brisbane city, an oasis if you will. The reception needed to be held elsewhere, and for the couple, it was love at first sight when they walked into The Calile. The impressive architecture, the design, and ambiance was a contrast to their ceremony location, in all the right ways.

The wedding was inspired by the color palette from both the contrasting venues and the season. For anyone unfamiliar with a Brisbane winter, it feels the same as an autumn day for most. Oranges, sandstones, greens, and touches of gold the perfect blend to set the tone.

For Kira, there was a short-lived fixation with creating her own arbor. With an idea of a feature hexagon arbor in mind, Kira took to the internet for DIY instructions - how hard could it really be? After a lot of time spent on Google and Youtube, pages of notes, multiple trips to a local hardware store, and seven or so hours of intensive work, it just wasn't quite right. Turned out, the wedding stylist had one, ready to go, all along. Crisis averted.

Anne and Kira decided that spending the night together before the big day was best. They both sleep better next to one another and expecting to have a restless night with excited nerves, it was best to at least have the comfort of one another. In the morning, the separated, spent time with their families, and got ready.

They opted out of a pre-ceremony reveal, and instead kept true to the tradition of first seeing one another when they met at the aisle. Procession order wasn't a hard choice. They had decided early in their relationship that whoever had the courage to propose would choose the last name they would take. Since Kira had proposed, and Anne was to take Kira's name, it made sense to have Anne walk towards Kira at the altar as a symbol of taking her last name.

After being pronounced married, they head back to the Calile, where the room already had an incredible vibe. There were speeches, there were tears, and there were lots of questionable dance moves thrown onto the dance floor. It was everything that Anne and Kira had dreamt it would be.

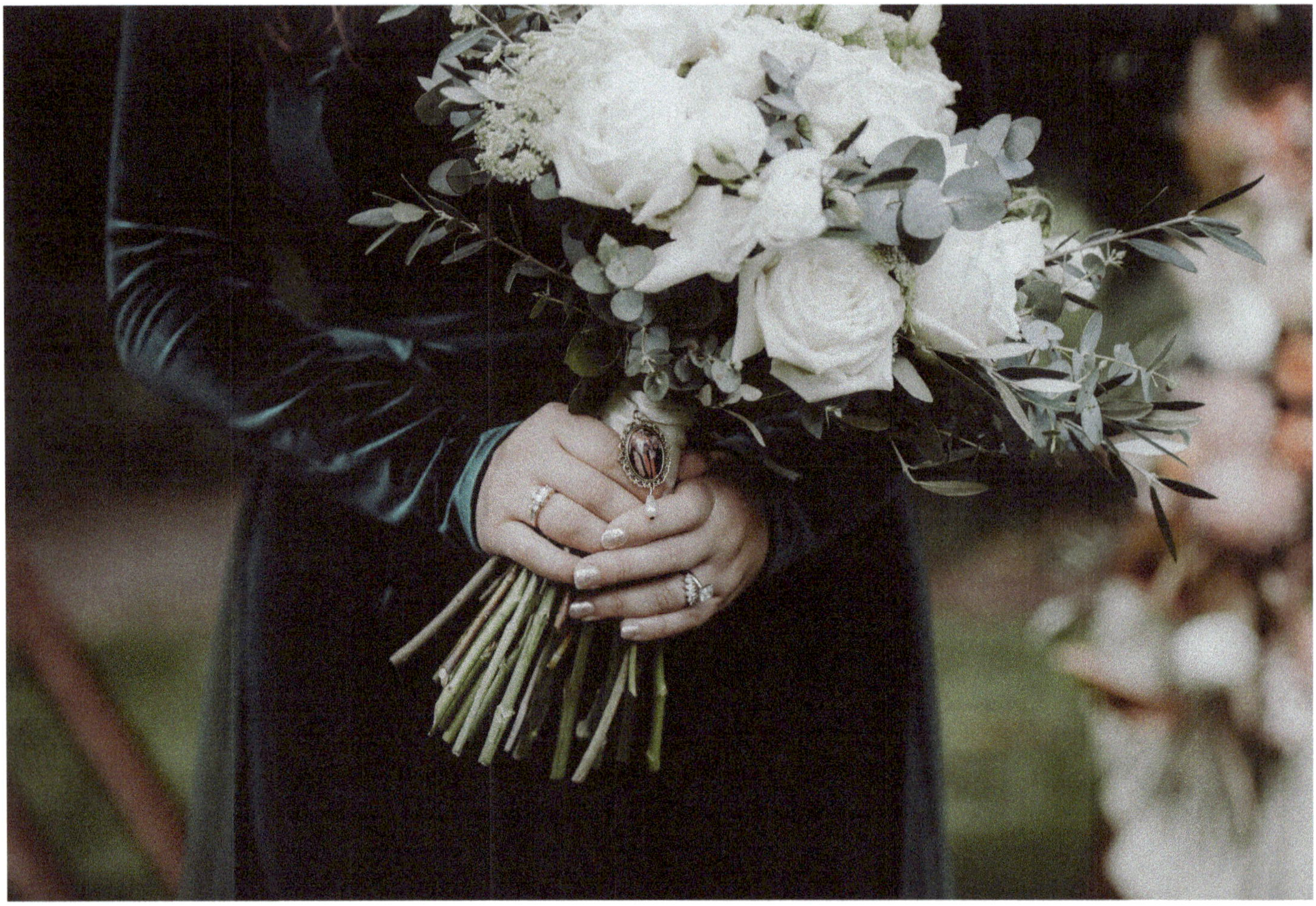
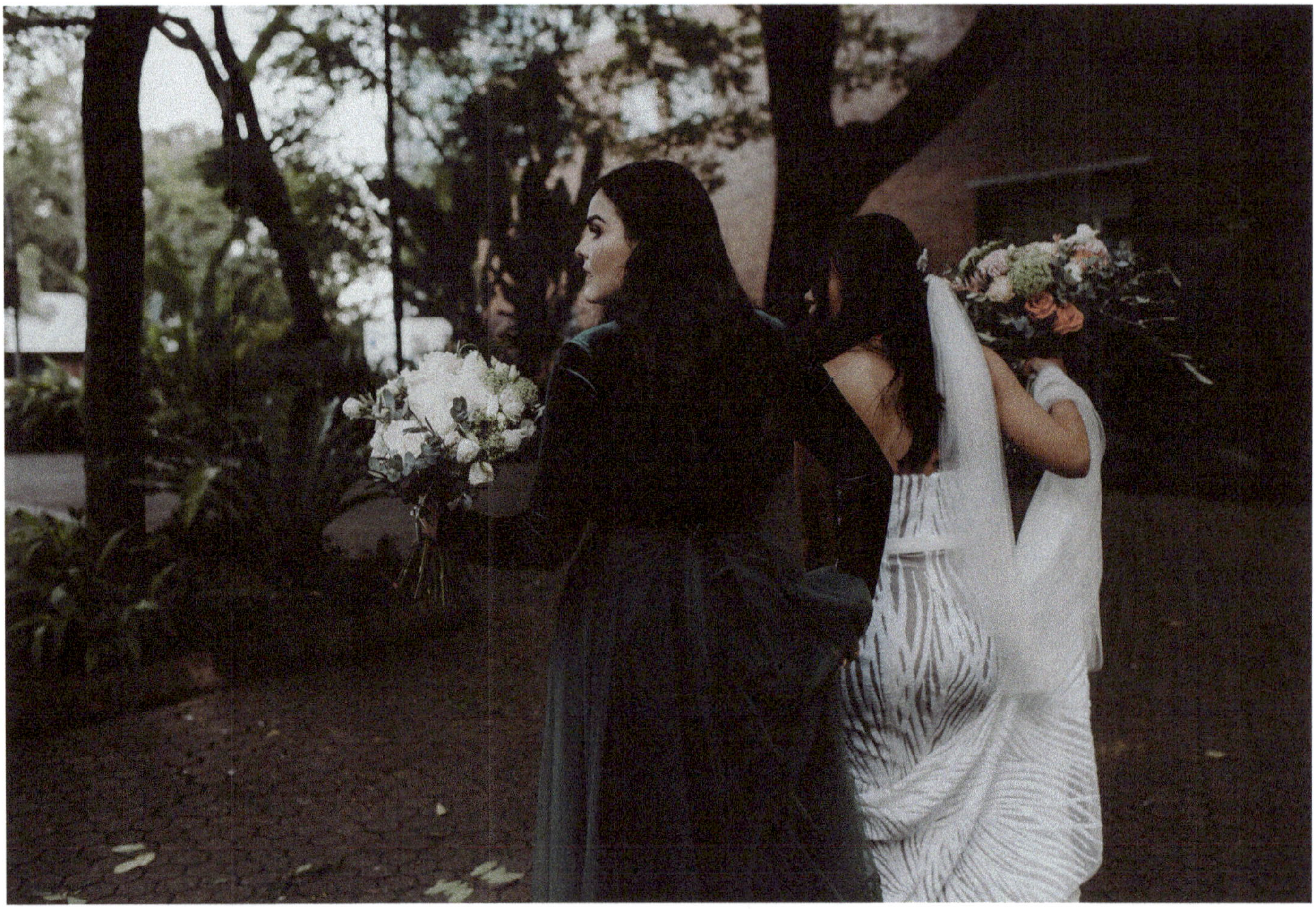

Accessories Ruby & Sage | **Cake** Nodo | **Catering** The Calile | **Celebrant** Josh Withers | **Ceremony** Tayla Mae | **Ceremony Venue** The Gardens Club
Event Planner & Florist Borrowed Events, Inspired By Love Events | **Engagement Rings** Diamondport | **Gown Designer** J'adore, Shieke, Elle Zeitoune
H&MU Sarah Neill, Kate Devlin | **Photographer** Lightsmith Images | **Reception Music** Kyle Bryant | **Reception Venue** The Calile | **Signage** Blank Space
Collective | **Transport** Limoso | **Wedding Favours** Charity Donations In Memoriam Of Their Grandmothers

MEET, AMANDA AFTON PHOTOGRAPHY

Contributed by Amanda Afton, Amanda Afton Photography
www.amandaaftonphotography.com

Who is Amanda, tell us a little bit about you!
Honest, no-bullshit. A delicate balance of charismatic and awkward AF. Fairly tomboyish and struggling to get past the classic T-shirt and mom jeans combo. Not excellent at expressing emotion, but I'll often bust a tear or two during the vows. My current endeavors include trying to keep plants and herbs alive, living a healthy, rounded lifestyle, and learning how to cook more than tacos and pasta.

What sparked your interest in becoming a wedding photographer?
My love for being behind a camera and my absolute boredom with taking landscape or architectural photos. There's a certain nostalgia to capturing people in a brief moment in time. When I realized how much I loved going through our old family albums [I still do every time I go home], I knew I should pursue it. Wedding photography allows me to play a small part in that cycle, freezing a moment for you to come back to years later.

What do you love most about being able to capture weddings and engagements?
Honestly, it's always all about the people. I love that people trust me to tell a narrative for them, finding people that I connect with well enough to get what they're all about. I would have little to no love for photography if it weren't for the people in the photos.

What is a typical day for Amanda Afton Photography?
It's far from glamorous, and it's a bit unstructured at the moment.

I wake up around eight, have a slow breakfast and coffee, then meander to my desk in my trackies and spend the rest of the day shifting between editing, e-mails, and Instagram, and every couple days tweaking my already perfectly functional website. My chiro tells me I need to get up more during the day and drink more water instead of coffee, but it's a work in progress. I love being at weddings and being with people, but shooting a full wedding is such a socially and mentally "on" activity, being still and solitary in my own space for most of the week is a necessary creative recharge.

Give us your top three tips for a couple, when looking to book a photographer.
One: Find a photographer who you connect with, at some level. Your photographer, unlike most of your other wedding vendors, spends almost the whole day with you and needs to feel some sense of connection in order to tell a story that's unique to you and your celebration.

Two: Look for a photographer whose work gets you excited! You'll have your wedding photos forever, and loving their work means you'll connect with your images for years to come.

Three: Do a little bit of extra research and look at full wedding days. Blogs usually give you a better idea of how the whole day will look, while Instagram can be incredibly curated. Make sure your photographer has your back in all different lighting situations and can document your memories during even the chaotic parts of the day.

Lastly, is there a wedding that you've photographed that will stay with you always? Tell us about it.
Honestly, no, there's not one. There are parts of weddings that will stay with me always! Anytime a couple walks down the aisle together, little kiddos who get to be there when parents get married, certain couples who tell me they hate being in photos and are so madly into each other they couldn't give two shits about me being there, that one story in the speeches that probably shouldn't have been told, among others.

I wouldn't even feel right remembering one couple's story above all the others, because they're all so beautifully unique, but I love remembering the best parts of each one.

DEE & SARAH

PHOTOGRAPHY BY CORI TAYLOR PHOTOGRAPHY
www.coritaylor.com

CALIFORNIA, USA

Dee and Sarah made a joint decision to get engaged. Sarah wanted a traditional diamond engagement ring, and Dee a wooden ring to have as her engagement ring, and a different ring for her wedding band. Together they went to a local jeweler and picked out the diamond ring. Dee had secretly asked to tell Sarah that the ring would be ready two weeks after it actually was - it gave her just enough time to plan a surprise proposal.

And, on a typical Saturday morning, while walking their dog Moose, Dee popped the question. Sarah, through tears of joy, exclaimed, 'yes!'

Dee had organized for friends to set up a 'just engaged' romantic brunch for two at their home while they were out - a complete surprise to Sarah once they returned home. Sarah had already gotten a ring for Dee, and although she thought she needed more time to plan something, it just felt right. In their kitchen at home got down on one knee and spoke from the heart.

The decision to elope wasn't the first to come to mind. Dee and Sarah were engaged in September and started looking at local wedding venues in October. There weren't plans to buy a home together until the most perfect Cape Cod style home appeared on Zillow. They closed the house in November and essentially depleted their entire savings account.

When they started to talk about wedding options a few months later, the various options they came up with just didn't sit right. The lovers both had family spread across the United States that would need to travel, and there was an uneasiness towards building up their savings for several years only to spend it all again on one single day.

So, Dee and Sarah decided to elope while on vacation in California.

Telling their parents of their plans was easy, although endowed with nerves. Dee knew that her Mom had always dreamt of seeing her daughter walk down the aisle. They each told their parents before the wedding and told friends and family in the days that followed the wedding before sharing the news on social media. The outpouring of love and congratulations was immense; there was not an ounce of dissapointment.

The entire elopement was kept pretty simple and low key. They had a slow morning together, enjoyed coffee on the porch, and took in what the day was about to bring. When hair and makeup arrived, Dee and Sarah said goodbye to each other and strategically stayed in opposite ends of their Airbnb. They sent each other several letters throughout the day, and Dee had flowers and Sarah's favorite Starbucks drink delivered too.

With their best friends, they arrived at the beach separately and met up with their photographer and officiant, who arranged the first look.

Shortly after, the ceremony began.

Right before Dee read her vows, she pulled two handkerchiefs out of her pocket, on for each of them that read, "for your happy tears - Sara and Deanna 7.30.19." Dee lead with her vows, stating that when she started falling in love with Sarah that first summer she had asked her to, 'meet me in another universe' because she couldn't imagine a world where they could be together. They both had struggled through discovering their sexuality together when they first met. She proudly expressed that she was so glad they had the courage to fall in love with each other and make that universe a reality.

Bow Tie Express | **Ceremony Venue** La Jolla Shores | **Celebrant** Dream Beach Wedding | **Engagement & Wedding Rings** Murduff's Jewelry Store
Florist Dream Beach Wedding | **Gown Designer** LuLu's | **H&MU** Just Lago | **Pants** Brooks Brothers | **Photographer** Cori Taylor Photography | **Reception Venue** Galaxy Taco | **Shirt** Brooks Brothers | **Suspenders** Macy's | **Transport** Stay Classy Transportation

HOW TO SAVE YOUR WEDDING PARTY MONEY
It's an honor, but it can be expensive

So you've decided that you want to have a wedding party and you've selected the handful of people that you couldn't imagine marrying the love of your life without being by your side. You've popped thought up the most perfect way to ask them to be a part of your big day. And they say, yes!

A few months down the track, they come to you and let you know that while they are honored that you've asked them to be a part of your day, they're really worried that they can't afford it.

And it is a valid response. The wedding party is putting in the hours to make your day come to life and then on top of that, and they are often lugged with a few extra things that they can't afford; dresses, shoes, hair and makeup, a bach party...the list goes on.

So, before you have to have any awkward conversations, here are a few things you can do to help reduce those costs that fall back on your favorite people.

Be flexible with their outfits
Mismatched wedding party attire is a trend that is here to stay; make use that! Let your wedding party choose their own outfits. If you want to stipulate a color palette, do that, but let your people choose something that is within their budget and something that they could get more use out of than just the one day.

This one also extends to shoes. Pick a color, and let people do their own shopping!

The best part about being flexible on attire, it'll mean that your wedding party will all feel comfortable and confident in what they're wearing on the day- and you won't have to worry about finding attire that suits all the body shapes that make up your wedding party.

Make professional hair and makeup optional
Professional hair and makeup can usually cost a whole lot more that you might anticipate, generally somewhere between $100-$200 per person, and that can be a lot of cash for some people!

If you've got someone that is handy with a foundation brush or the curling wand, then maybe having them help out is a good idea. Or, just let everyone do their hair and makeup themselves on the day.

Try to cut down on travel and accommodation costs
There will probably be a few dates where your wedding party will need to show up; the engagement party, the outfit choosing, the bach party, the rehearsal, etc. and that generally translates to money spent on travel and accommodation options.

Also, let people know well in advance if they will need to travel, so they have the opportunity to get plane tickets and a bed to sleep in at a good price.

If you can, try and group together different events, do that! Maybe you could plan a trip to try on outfits the day after your engagement party? Or, the bach party could be the night before you have your wedding rehersal?

Say no to wedding gifts
After the planning, after they've brought an outfit and pulled together an epic bach party, and stood beside you on a very important day, it'd almost seem unfair to also expect a wedding gift from them.

While there will be some people who feel guilty about showing up without a gift in hand, assure them that their presence is your present, that they have already gone above and beyond and that you don't expect anything more.

ETICA

EVENTS

Destination Events in South America

www.eticaevents.com

I love the way you smile. I love the way your hands feel wrapped around my body. I love the way you feel like home. I love your eyes. I love how thoughtful you are. I love how much fun we have together. I love the way we communicate. I love how much we challenge one another to be better versions of ourselves. I love it when you tickle me to sleep. I love that we have created our own meaning of what family is. I love that we dream of a future side by side. I love that we have built a home together. I love the way you look at me and embrace me when I get home from work. I love that I've never laughed like I have with you. I love it when we cook together. I love that you are patient. I love that you are kind. I love that you care so much about the people who you love most. I love the way that you read my mind. I love the feeling I get when you call me just to say hello. I love that we miss one another, even if it has only been a few hours apart. I love that there is never judgment. I love that you push me to achieve more than I ever thought I could. I love that you believe in me. I love the little wrinkles around your eyes when you smile. I love our dreams are in line. I love that I am supported. I love the way you fold up my clothes. I love that you inspire me. I love that I can just be myself around you. I love that you make me feel safe. I love all these things and more about you. I want to always walk by your side in life. I love you. Will you marry me?

TO THE MOON AND BACK

KIRSTEN & JEN

I decided that I wanted to surprise Jen with a proposal on our one year anniversary because it was the only way I could plan something and it not seem suspicious. I let her know that I was planning an awesome anniversary celebration with dinner and a show. I made an appointment for her hair, nails and make up [I knew she would have killed me if I did not make sure her mani was fresh!] and the anniversary was a great cover.

I went to meet Jen's parents to ask for their blessing, and once I had that I went straight to planning. I wanted to have the proposal be intimate with just us but I knew that Jen would want our friends and family close by. The Huntington Beach Pier on a Saturday was a perfect way to disguise our friends and family but still giving them a great view of 'the show'.

I had been watching the weather for weeks leading up to the day since it was happening on the beach. 24 hours before the proposal a random thunder and lightning storm came out of nowhere. IT DID NOT STOP raining for the entire day before and into Saturday. I was checking my weather app every minute, so worried it would ruin all of the plans. My mom bought a canopy tent as a backup plan and they had it over our picnic set up to protect it from the rain.

I had all of our closest friends [many who flew in from out of town to be there to celebrate with us] helping get the set-up complete. I put together my vision of this beautiful boho beach picnic right next to the lifeguard tower. My dad built the picnic table, my college roommates made an amazing cheese board and set up the picnic, my brother, sister and mom were raking the sand, moving the trash cans so they would be out of our view and removing the seaweed so the beach would be picture perfect. I also had a videographer and photographer pretending to be people on the beach so they could capture the 'yes' moment.

It stopped raining five minutes before Jen and I showed up and it was the most epic sunset of all time. It still gives me chills just thinking about it.

Photography: Brogan Jessup Photography

KATHLEEN & JESS

The planning process was definitely a secret. Despite being an unconventional relationship for both of our religious families, we still value some aspects of a traditional proposal and marriage. We had discussed a future and family, so it only felt natural that choosing marriage was the next step for us.

The original proposal plan didn't quite come to fruition. Let's just say that I'd planned for it to consist of a lady shaman, clay massage, and a picnic on a beautiful clear-blue private cenote with optional paddle boarding. Cut to us stuck at a mezcal bar in the thick of a thunderstorm, Kathleen yelling, "This thunderstorm is so beautiful!" and me simultaneously looking out toward the road closures. Funny isn't quite the word.

Despite the unexpected turn in the weather, Tulum was the perfect place to propose. We love the beautifully rustic yet boho-chic lifestyle of the community in Tulum. We had frequented those white sand beaches and fell in love with them repeatedly. It's been our go-to oasis for years.

On the last day of our vacation, our breakfast table happened to be where we sat the first time we ever visited Tulum. It just felt right and natural, just like our love!

The ring belonged to Kathleen's Grandmother. It was imperative for us to have family involvement and blessing from our parents. Coming out to our families was met with no shortage of contention, so the ring will always be a symbol of progress and unconditional love.

The engagement was a way to reinforce our commitment and love, both to ourselves and to our family and friends. It was followed by a huge outpouring of love and excitement. Not only are we finding that the engagement has given us the opportunity [and excuse!] to delve into quality memories we've shared, but we've enjoyed a fair few engagement celebrations along the way.

Photography: Chasewild

ASHLEY & CHLOE

We've been together for four years, and we met while working at Subway when we were 15 and 16 years old! I distinctly remember showing up for work and noticing this cute new girl- we took an order together and clicked instantly. We were so young, neither of us knew that we were anything other than straight, but we've been inseparable ever since.

Since we are still quite young, it was certainly a discussion as to whether or not we wanted to wait until we were older, more financially stable, etc., before we looked to get married. Early on in our relationship Chloe called 'dibs' on proposing, whenever it was to happen. Once we started living on our own together, it felt like a natural next step, and we definitely discussed it often.

Many people have a certain idea of what the ring should cost or should look like, but after giving it some thought, we decided just to pick our favorite ones [within reason- we didn't want to break the bank!]. At one point, the salesperson even suggested that we go for the more expensive option because our 'boyfriends' were paying - the joys of being stereotyped! Our rings actually ended up being on the less expensive side, and we feel that they are just as beautiful as their pricier alternatives.

Once we felt we were on the same page about waiting or not waiting, we went shopping and purchased our rings together.

After that point, I had no hand in the planning and let Chloe take the reins. We decided there would still be a bit of a surprise, as I knew it would be coming but didn't know when.

Chloe proposed in the living room of our apartment, and this was really special. We moved into our first home together in March, and it has definitely become our happy place, so it was really sweet to me that she chose to propose there. I feel like there is a lot of pressure to choose somewhere extravagant or adventurous, but this felt so much more 'us.'

Photography: April Evelyn Photography

LAUREN & TAYLOR

Photography: Samantha Lowe Photo

Lo was working on an elopement wedding at the Grand Canyon, and I got to tag along. I figured I might as well take advantage of the trip; we had a few days to explore after Lo was done with work.

I had the ring hidden in my backpack, and normally Lo doesn't get anything out of my bag because she claims I am a mess, and she can't find anything. We stopped at the infamous Whataburger, and it was packed, so we ate outside. It was a bit chilly, and I had a jacket in my bag, so Lo offered to get it out. I had a mini freak out and insisted she couldn't look in my bag. She saw an Amazon order from a few weeks before that I wouldn't let her see, so she just assumed she had a small gift in there. Disaster avoided.

When we went to a lookout point at the Grand Canyon to take some photos Lo had no idea what 'the money shot' meant until she finally looked down and saw the ring. She had no idea it was coming, and her face was priceless.

I would always joke that she was engaged and I had a girlfriend. So she stepped up to the plate and about six weeks later insisting that we needed another photo strip from the photo booth to add to our collection. She was acting weird but, I had no idea until on the second photo she whipped out a ring and asked me to be her wife. I was shocked!

We were planning a big wedding with all of our family and friends; however, it quickly became overwhelming. When Lo got the call to work a friend's wedding in Utrecht, Holland, we decided to make a wedding out of it.

We took our wedding budget and planned an epic 18-day trip through Europe. We had a private ceremony with just us and a photographer and spent the day running around the city. We finished the night sipping champagne while we watched the Eiffel Tower sparkle. Technically we are already married, but we'll be celebrating with a big reception sometime next year- surrounded by all our favorite people.

LOVE IN THE MOUNTAINS

PHOTOGRAPHY BY MCKENZIE BIGLIAZZI PHOTOGRAPHY
www.mckenziebigliazzi.com

Bridal Boutique Amanda's Bridal and Tux | **Florals** The Faux Bouquet | **Location** Garden of the Gods | **Lovers** Chelsea & Madi

CYDNEY & JORDAN
PHOTOGRAPHY BY HENRY TIEU PHOTOGRAPHY
www.henry-tieu.com

WASHINGTON, USA

vows
vows
JK
CL

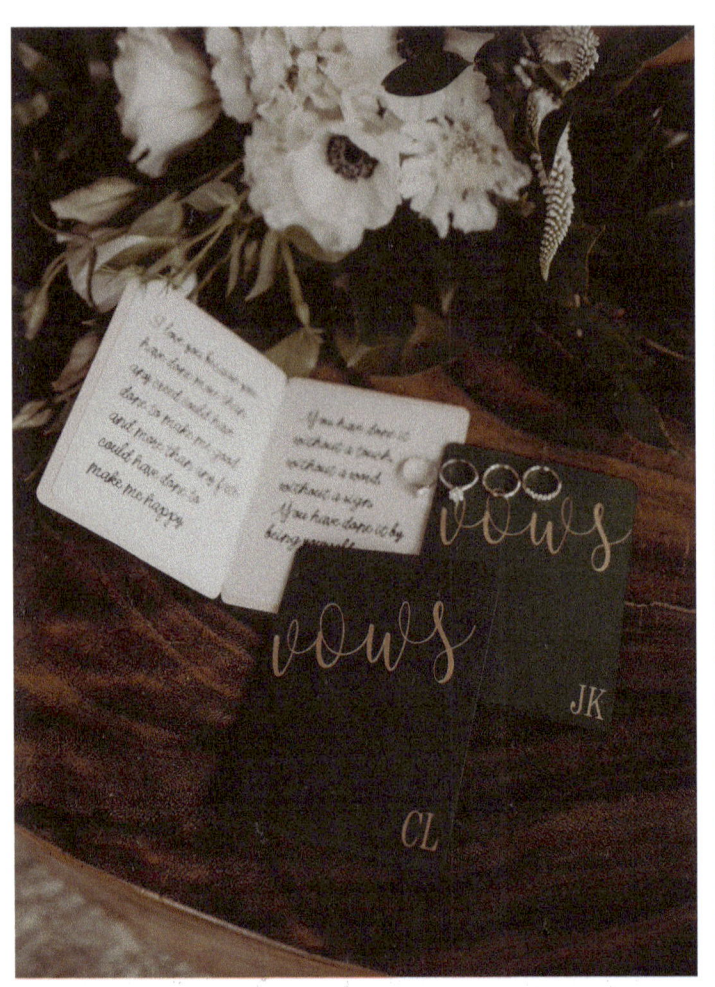

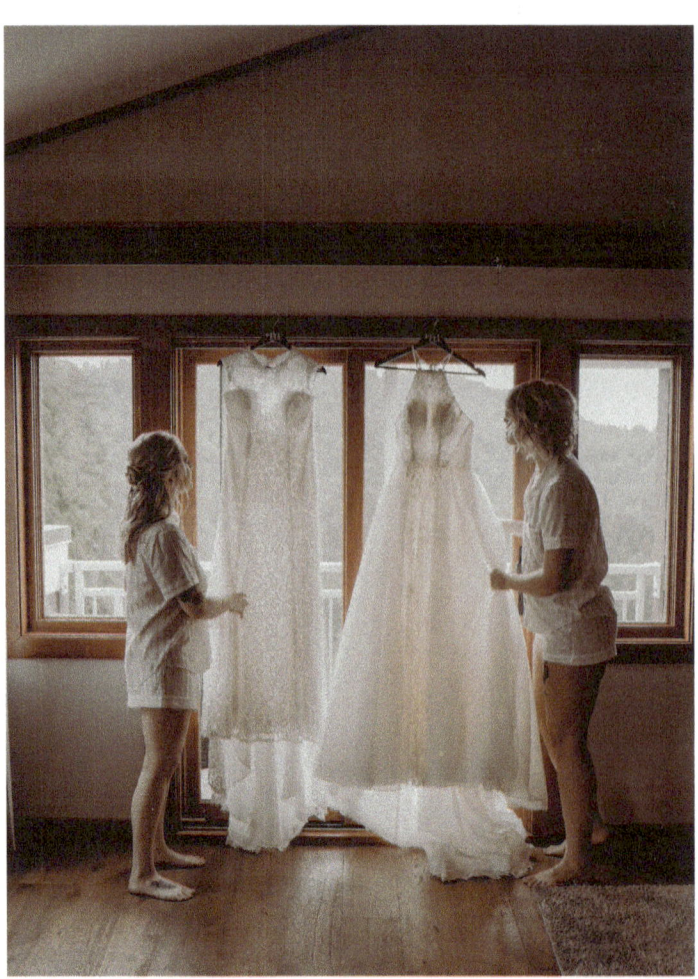

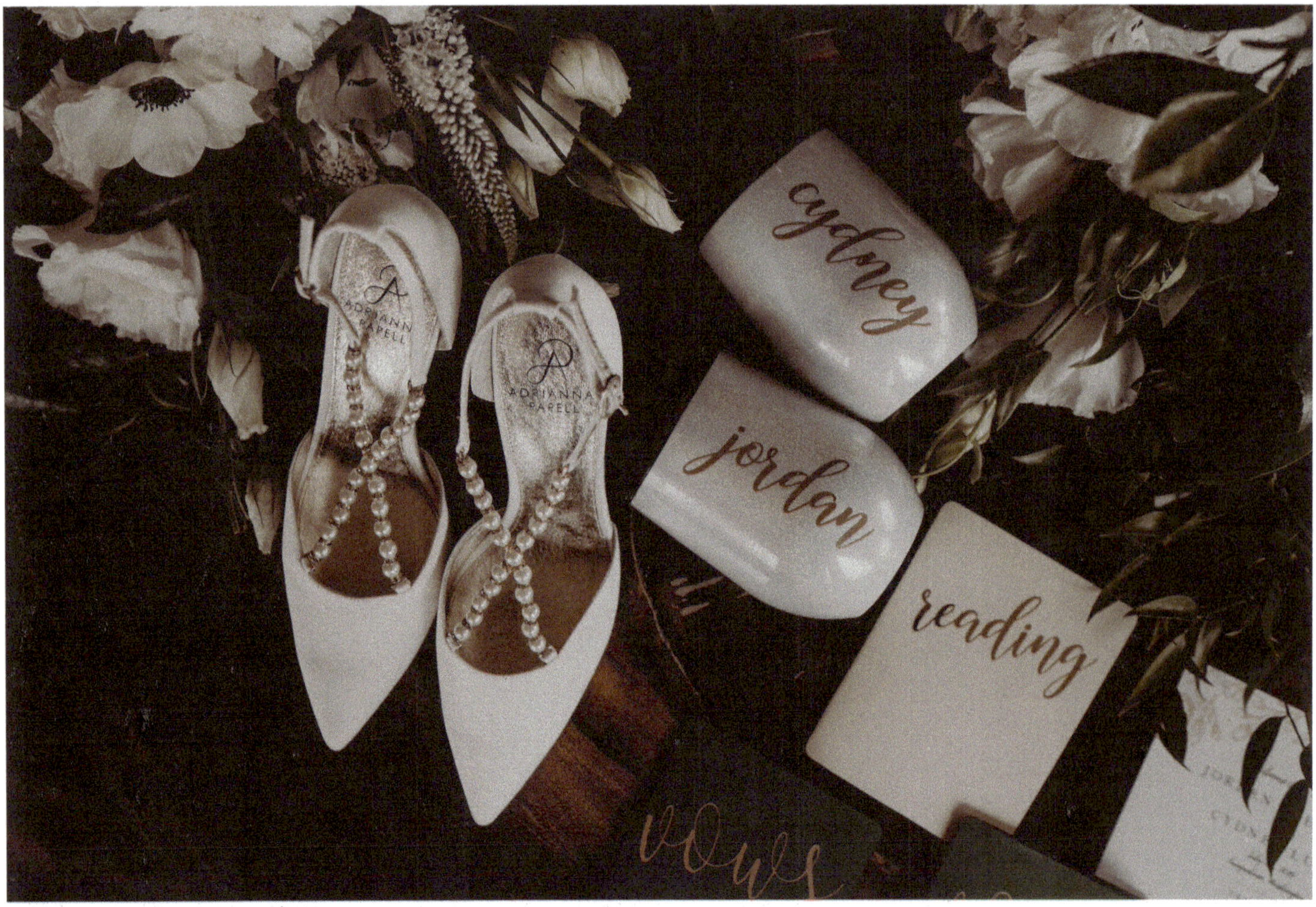
ADRIANNA PAPELL
cydney
jordan
reading
vows

Cydney and Jordan had only just moved to Seattle when they started to plan their wedding. Salish Lodge was the first and the last place they visited. Once they saw the view right on top of Snoqualmie Falls, they knew that the venue was perfect.

With a simplistic but elegant style in mind, Jordan got to the DIY projects. She hand-lettered on marble tiles to serve as table settings and on an empty photo frame sketched a welcome sign. She made books where they wrote their vows and tags and labels for their wedding favors [which was honey from the hives at the venue]. Her favorite project was a little corsage collar she made for their dog.

When it came to finding the perfect outfits, Cydney and Jordan wanted to share the experience. They both come from conservative states and weren't sure what to expect when they went shopping together for gowns - but the experience was nothing short of wonderful. They were welcomed into the bridal salon with open arms.

Having shopped together for gowns, it meant that their outfits complemented one another perfectly.

On the wedding day, things didn't go to plan.

The day started out slowly. The brides got ready together, had their hair and makeup done, and soaked in the enormity of what the day ahead held.

The ceremony went by in a blur. Childhood friends, siblings and Cydney's Grandfather all made memorable speeches- there wasn't a dry eye in the room.

Before heading out for sunset pictures below the waterfall with their photographer, Henry, they enjoyed some food with their favorite people.

Laughing, as brand new wives, newly married, they started the hike down to the falls. They spent the rest of the afternoon light taking all the photos that they'd been dreaming about since that first visit to the venue.

And, as soon as the sun set, things didn't quite go as expected.

Cydney, Jordan, and Henry found themselves lost hiking back up Snoqualmie Falls in the dark. Taking the mishap in their stride, they hiked through the mud for hours laughing at their misfortune. It was undoubtedly a memorable way to start their marriage.

There final memories of the wedding day are walking back up to their room after finally making their way back to the venue, covered in mud, to find each of their Maid of Honors asleep on the floor next to their wedding gifts- next to the dinner they had missed out on enjoying.

They had missed their entire reception.

And while a lot of people would feel devastated, Cydney and Jordan took it in their stride. They're both really glad that they chose to have an intimate, small ceremony with only close family and friends. They are thankful that they have the memories of seeing the faces of those they love the most, beaming towards them with love and joy while they shared their vows.

To Cydney and Jordan, their wedding felt like their day, not an event that was planned for a bunch of guests. A true celebration of their commitment to one another. Although they may joke that their marriage is a business arrangement, in actuality, marriage is nothing but an enriched version of the loving partnership that Cydney and Jordan have developed over the last six years together.

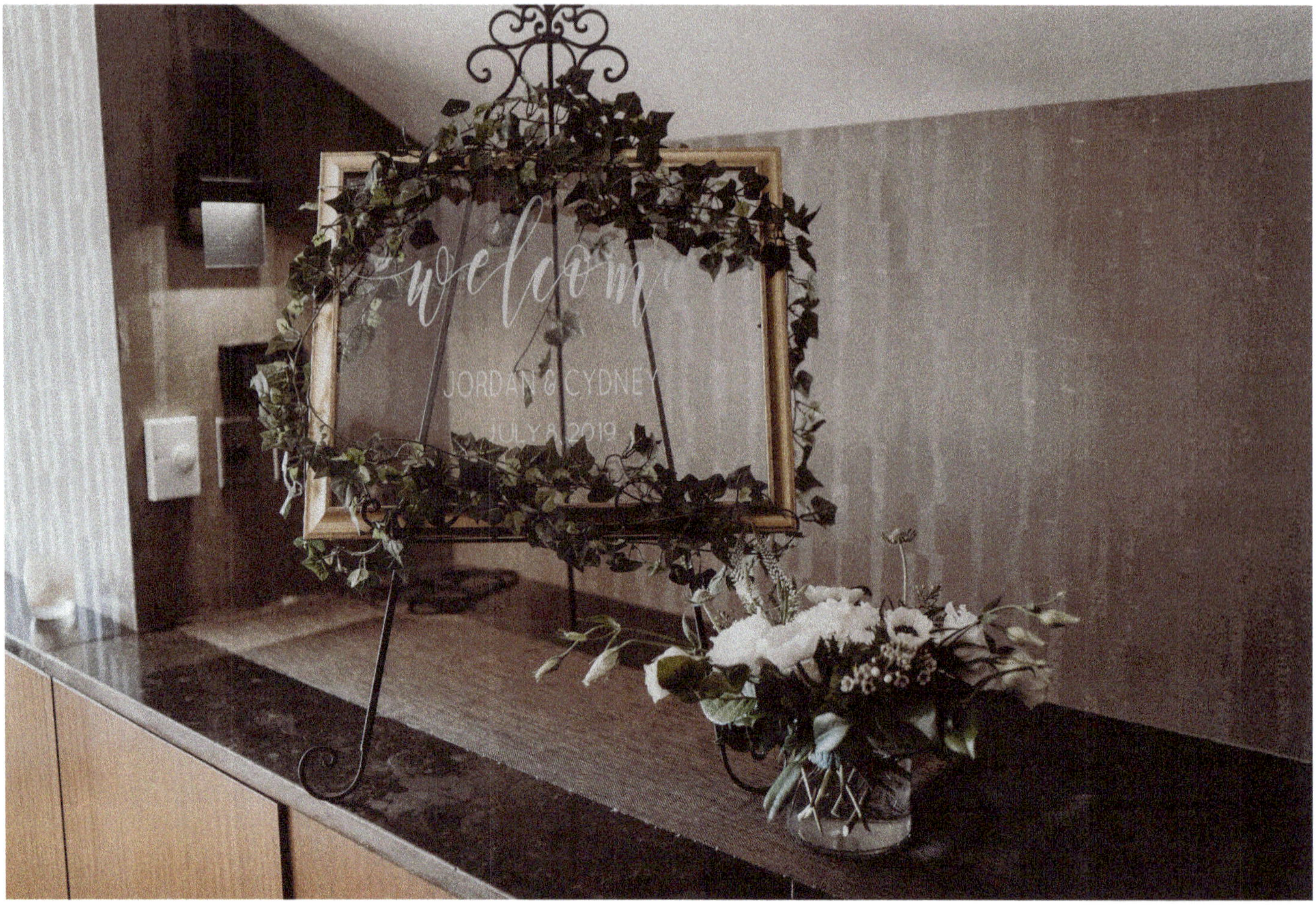
welcom
JORDAN & CYDNEY
JULY 8, 2019

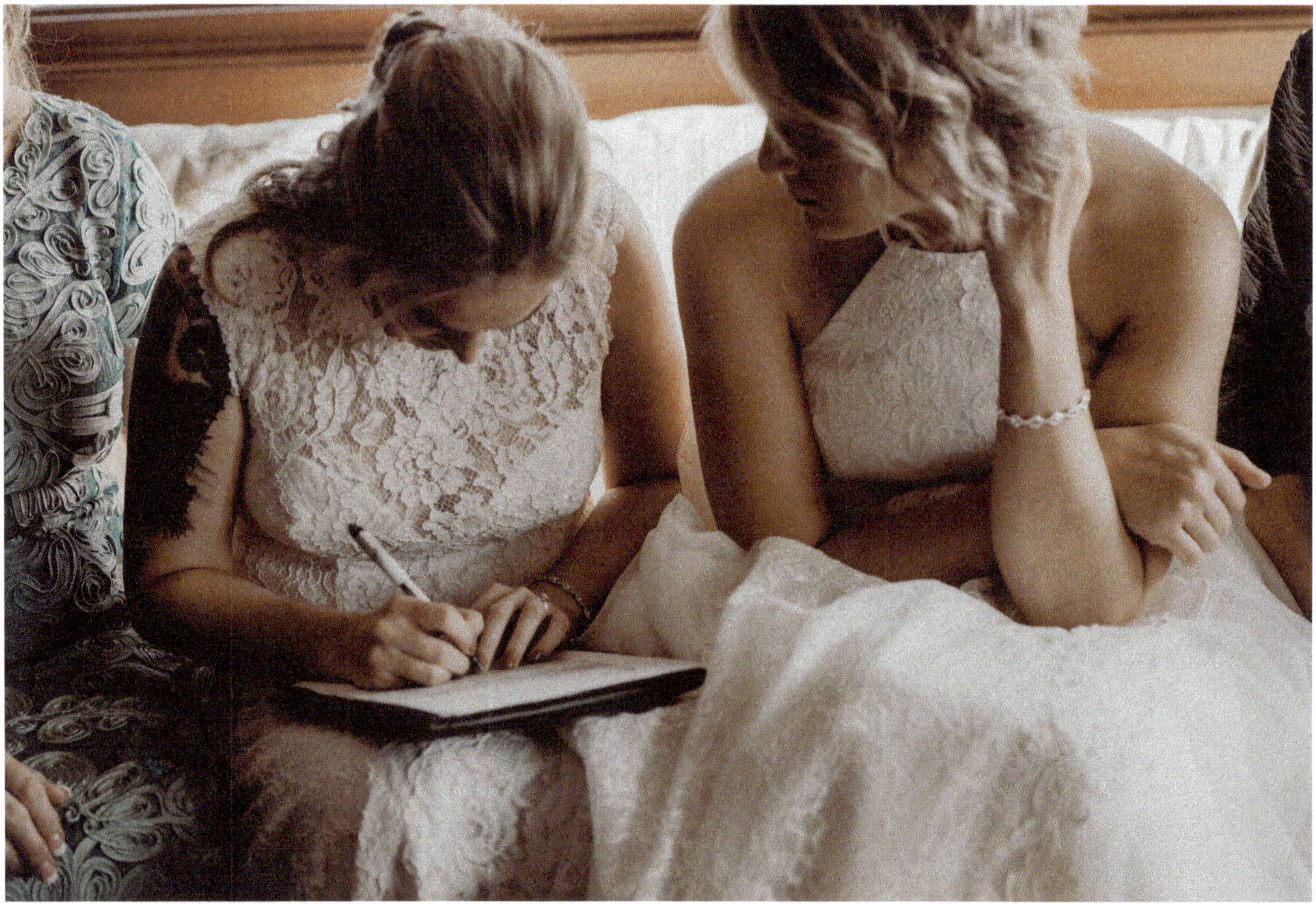

Accessories Ross-Simons, Givenchy | **Catering** Salish Lodge and Spa | **Celebrant** Seattle Wedding Officiants | **Ceremony Venue** Salish Lodge and Spa
Engagement & Wedding Rings Helzberg Diamonds | **Florist** Down to Earth | **H&MU** Salon Maison | **Photographer** Henry Tieu | **Robes** Victoria's Secret

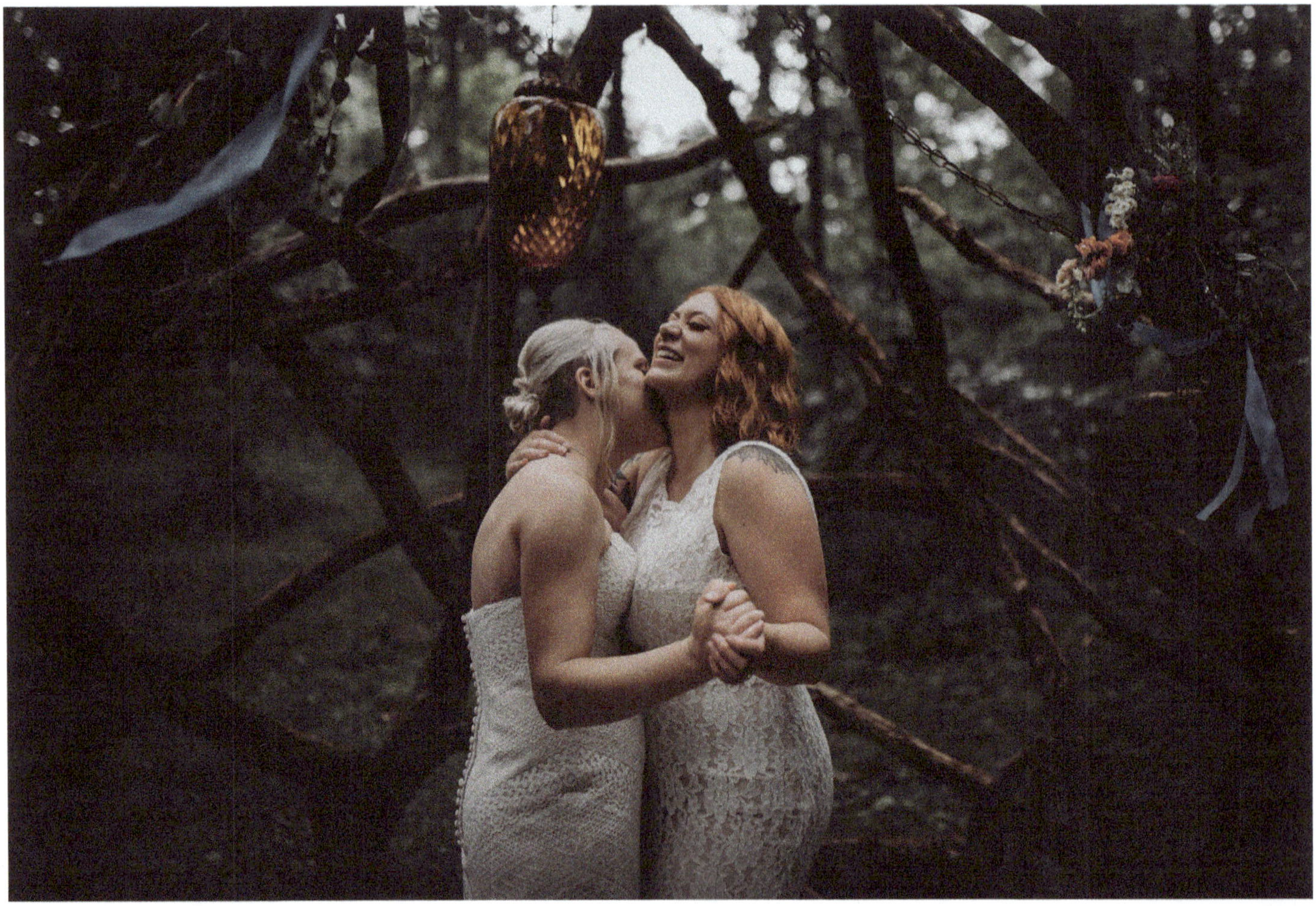

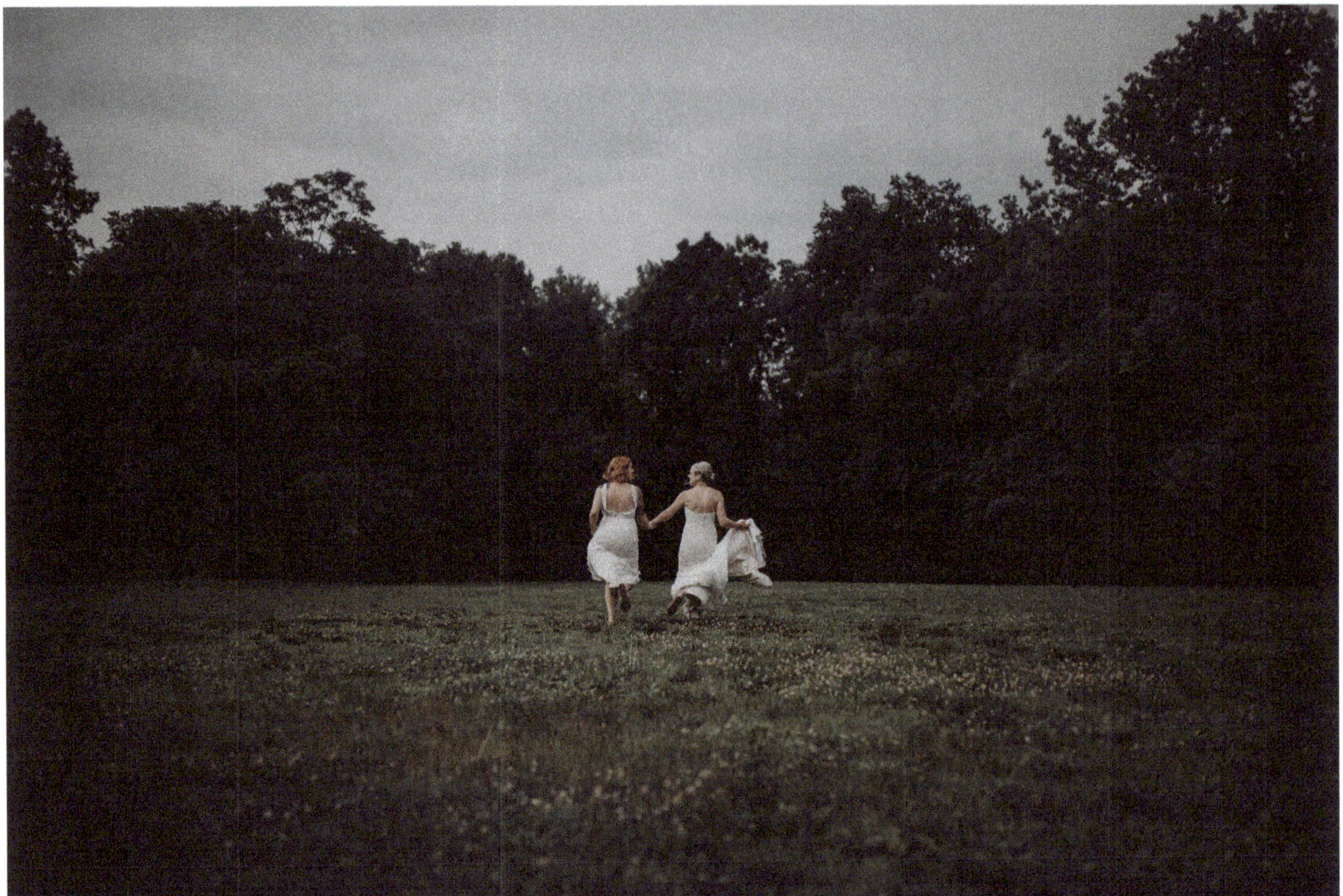

love freely, love wholly

PHOTOGRAPHY BY RAINWATER PHOTOGRAPHY
www.rainwater-photography.com

Corrie and Kelly didn't have a typical start to their relationship. They met through Corie's ex-girlfriend who happened to be a server at the same restaurant where Kelly was a chef.

They were friends for a while, then roommates - it made for a solid foundation. Before long, their true feelings bubbled to the surface.

Not too long after they began dating, strapped for cash, Corie borrowed an air mattress, brought $80 worth of sushi, and set up the living room floor with an epic picnic. They watched Star Trek and cuddled with their animals. It's a simple thing, but also one of their favorite memories together.

However, like all relationships, there have been ups, and there have been downs. For Corie, there haven't been many times during their five years together were they haven't felt like the sky was falling. Together they've lost family members, friends and fur babies, but they have always held strong together. Usually laughing; usually inappropriately.

There's been a lot of relearning and communication and plenty of undoing of toxic habits carried over from past relationships — all things that have built patience with one another and a strong foundation.

For Corie, it's Kelly's heart that is her favorite thing about her. She has never seen someone have so much compassion. Kelly makes a point to know the names of most of downtown's homeless population and always reminds them to be safe. Kelly's laugh is also one of the most genuine sounds Corie has ever known. Their friends frequently say, 'when Kelly laughs, you can tell down to her toenails that she thinks it's funny.'

For Kelly, it is Corie's assertiveness that is most attractive. It means that Kelly always knows exactly where she stands, which is something that she has never experienced in a relationship before. For the first time, Kelly is also experiencing a relationship where she feels wholly supported; Corie is always excited when she succeeds and feels comforted when things are hard.

This styled edit was put together by their wedding planner and happened around the time of their one-year anniversary.

HOW TO END YOUR WEDDING WITH A BANG

How couples who have been there did it

There is one part of the wedding night that you might not have even thought about yet, the moment that you leave. And while it isn't imperative to have a memorable send-off, it can be an awesome way to leave the party and walk into life as a married couple.

We asked a few couples who've been through it all what those final moments looked like for them.

Emma & Jane
This is going to sound a little ridiculous, but it is precisely what happened. Some of our wedding party used a temporary white spray paint, wrote 'just married' on the back of our car and attached strings of tin cans to our tow bar- just like the movies! When the night was winding up, we jumped in our car and drove away- making a huge noise wherever we went!

Brandy & Nic
We had all of our guests come together in two rows, create an arch, and we made our way through the middle while they blew bubbles over us and 'Love on Top' by Beyonce played. We had actually booked a room at the reception venue, so we made our way upstairs and called it a night.

Meagan & Martine
We had our DJ let all our guests know that it was the last dance of the night, and we got down and boogied with everyone! There was plenty of loud singing, an uncle got down and did the worm, and there were plenty of hugs and shoulder shimmies! Then, the lights came on, and we all jumped into the bus that we had booked for everyone and got off at our stop.

Amelia & Andie
We had seen so many images on social media of sparkler send-offs, and we loved the idea! We wanted our photographer to capture the moment, so we had the send-off and then went and thanked all of our guests for coming along and being a part of the festivities before slipping away in a cab.

Elise & Megan
We had about 104 guests at our wedding, and they proved themselves as quite good at partying! We were exhausted after such a gigantic day, but there were still plenty of guests kicking on, so we started making our way around thanking everyone for coming, and once we'd got to most guests, we snuck off and called an Uber. Honestly, no one has mentioned that they missed us leaving, but everyone is still talking about having the time of their lives!

Jo & Sara
We hadn't planned anything for a wedding exit; it just wasn't important to us. However, Sarah pulled the ultimate surprise on Jo and organized to have fireworks mark the end of the night! It was just as incredible as you'd imagine.

Amy & Sasha
We'd thought about a sparkler send-off, however, we were so pre-occupied partying that we totally forgot to do it! Looking back, it absolutely doesn't matter - we partied with our guests until 1 am when the venue kicked us out! Most of the guest caught themselves and Uber home, including us, and, of course, we stopped by McDonald's drive-thru before heading making it back to our hotel.

Hayley & Stevie
There was no grand exit necessary- we were quite literally the last ones on the dancefloor! We could have danced all night long but decided to call it quits before the sun came up and we stumbled over to our Airbnb just up the road from the venue.

KATIE & TAYLOR

PHOTOGRAPHY BY KENZ & NICK PHOTOGRAPHY
www.kenzandnickphoto.com

MINNESOTA, USA

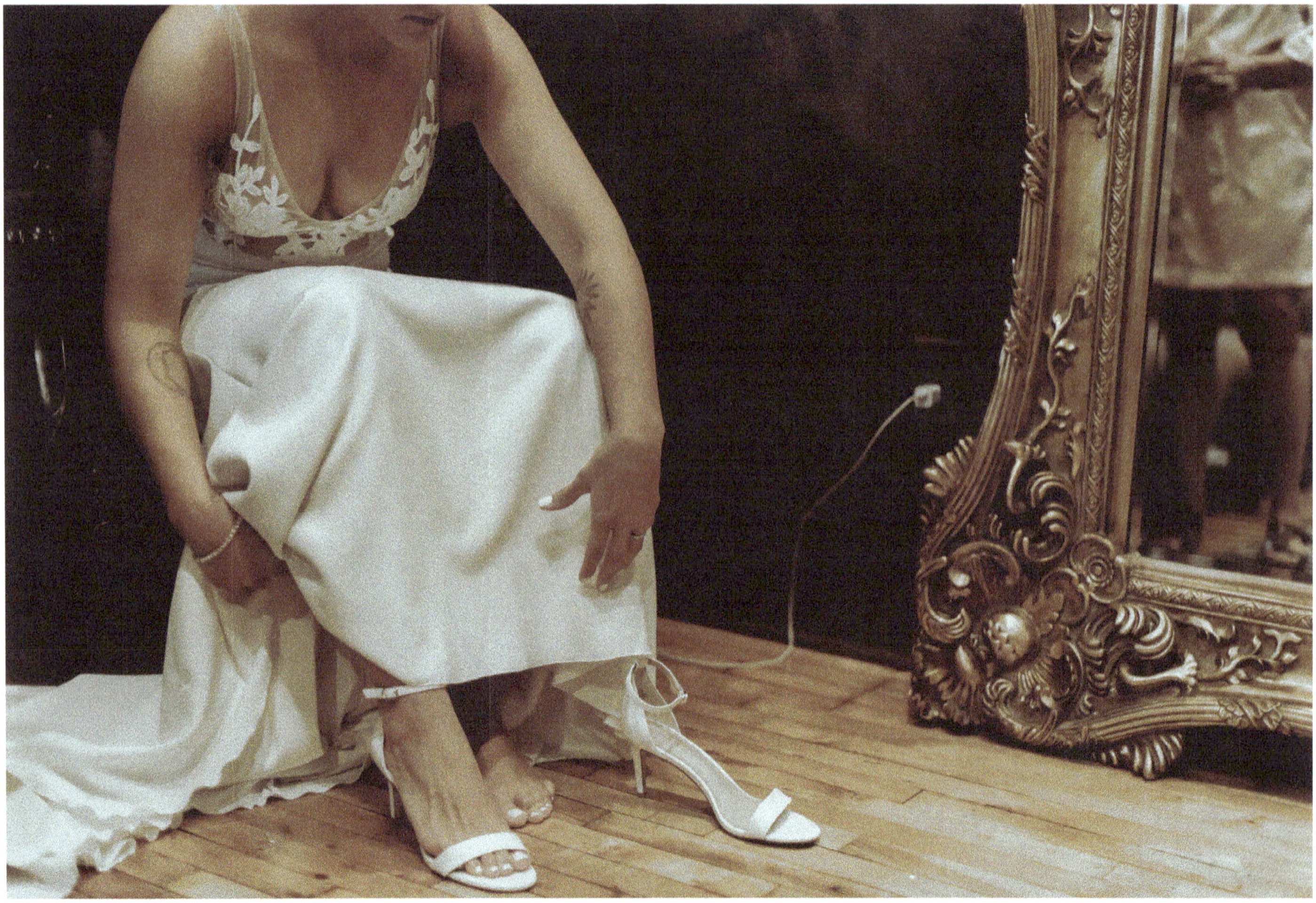

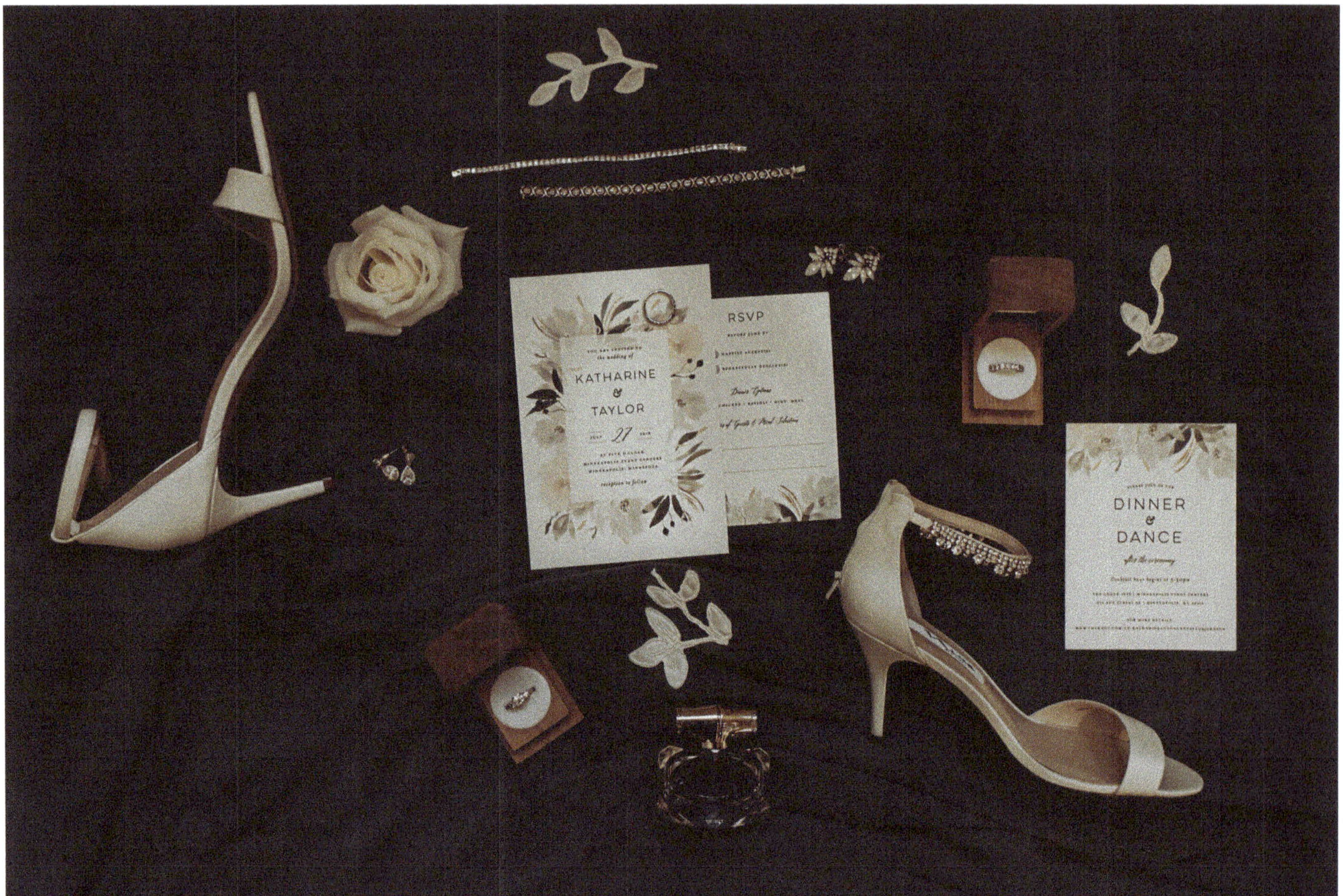
KATHARINE
&
TAYLOR
RSVP
DINNER
&
DANCE

These lovers met on Tinder in Minneapolis the summer before their senior year of college. Taylor was home for the summer working at an internship and Katie taking classes at the University of Minnesota. After their very first date, they were infatuated with each other and tried to hang out as much as possible throughout the summer before Taylor went back to school in Omaha.

They spent senior year of college taking turns driving six hours to visit one another. The day after graduation, Taylor moved back to Minneapolis to be with Katie. That was five years ago now.

Katie and Taylor had discussed, at length, that Katie would be the one to propose. Katie had planned to fly both sets of parents out to Denver so that they could all celebrate together over a weekend. However, the rings that they had been looking at together came a little sooner than expected, and a very impulsive Katie couldn't wait. She proposed to Taylor less than 24 hours later.

After a quiet morning together taking the dogs for a walk and doing some yard work, Katie ducked inside to grab the ring. She had planned a big speech but ended up crying and getting down on one knee while Taylor just looked in shock. She, of course, said 'yes.'

They still had that party with their families a little over a month later.

Wedding inspiration came from their venue, the Minneapolis Event Center. For the ceremony, there was already a big courtyard with a bunch of trees and plants, and the reception space was a big glass atrium. A few exposed beams were styled with greenery to create a rustic but modern vibe. Minimal, but it's all that was really needed.

When it came to finding dresses, they both began the search online. They each booked separate appointments at a&be Bridal, where Taylor fell in love with a gown off the rack, and Katie found the bodice of one dress to combine with a skirt from another to create a one-of-a-kind gown.

The night before the wedding, Katie and Taylor hosted a welcome event. It was an opportunity for everyone to get together, share some food and conversation over drinks. It was also an opportunity for the two brides to thank everyone for coming.

The wedding day couldn't have gone any better. Both brides got ready in separate rooms next door to one another. This meant that their families were able to come and go, and the anticipation of the first look mounted.

There were family portraits before the ceremony, and as the open bar opened, their nearest and dearest started to gather for the proceedings.

Katie's Uncle, Andy, officiated their ceremony. Both Katie and Taylor had written their own vows - they laughed, and they cried their way through them. It's safe to say, their love for one another was spilled over everyone in that space.

During the ceremony, Taylors Grandpa sang 'Granted' by Josh Groban, which allowed the lovers to look around at their guests and really soak up all the love in the room.

Once the ceremony concluded, they sat to eat dinner and had a Father-Daughter dance and their first dance as wife and wife. The newlyweds snuck away for a few photos to catch that sunset light, some of their favorite images to look back on and admire.

Heading back the venue, it was time to relax, grab a drink, and dance the night away in celebration of their new relationship status.

Accessories Untamed Petals, Sara Gabriel | **Bridal Boutique** a & bé bridal shop | **Catering** Minneapolis Event Cente | **Ceremony & Reception Venue** Minneapolis Event Center | **Celebrant** Andy Anton [Katie's Uncle] | **Event Planner & Stylist** Ashley Nelson | **Entertainment** Adagio Djay | **Engagement & Wedding Rings** Brilliant Earth | **Florist** EDG Productions, Taylor Jacobs | **Gown Designers** Rebecca Schoneveld, Emmy Mae Bridal | **H&MU** Primped MN, Andria Johnson, Jamie Arrington | **Photographer** Kenz & Nick Photography | **Shoes** The Wedding Shoppe, Men's Warehouse | **Stationery** Minted **Signage** EDG Productions, Taylor Jacobs

www.marilialimaphoto.com

THE LIST

SOME OF THE VERY BEST WEDDING VENDORS

AUSTRALIA | USA | AROUND THE WORLD

TAHNEE JADE PHOTOGRAPHY
Photography

Relaxed and natural documentary-style wedding photographer obsessed with candidly capturing real life love stories. Your wedding embodies all the stories you've shared so far, and starts the story of your future. Think of me as providing the beautiful, meaningful pictures for this chapter of YOUR story.

www.tahneejadephotography.com

SUPERBLOOM
Florist

Superbloom began in 2017 as an outgrowth of event designers The Style Co, which means the creation of good times is in our DNA. Despite the casual vibes, we're hopeless design geeks. Less flower children, and more flower engineers. We obsess over every brief and concept, creating maximum bang for bud.

www.superbloom.com.au

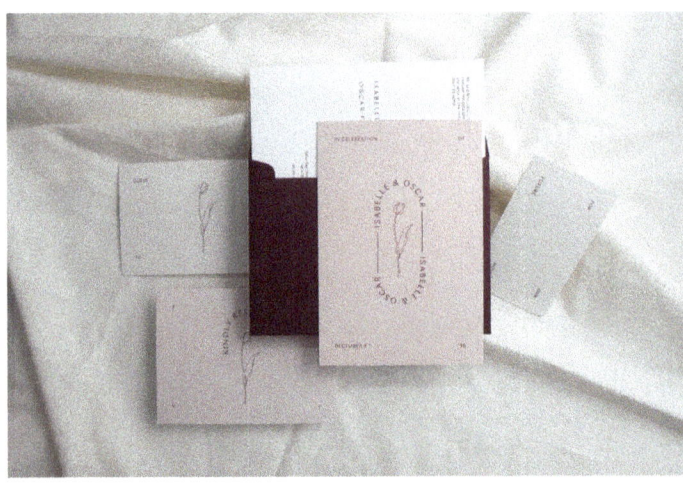

PAPER JEAN
Stationery

Paper Jean was born from a love of paper and refined design. We are passionate about sophisticated stationery for the contemporary couple. Our current collection serves to deliver a range of styles from romantic botanical elements to crisp typography. Let's begin your stationery conversation.

www.paperjean.com.au

IN AN INSTANT PHOTO BOOTH
Photo Booth

An open air photo booth offering sweet props, killer backdrops and best of all; pure sass. In An Instant is the dream team of sweet misfits turning your epic moments into the greatest of memories. Fact.

www.inaninstantphotobooth.com.au

AUSTRALIA

STUDIO CAKE ART
Cakes & Desserts

Studio Cake Art based in Melbourne's West is re-known for unconventional cake artistry. Christina and her kick-arse cake team meet with the couple to talk all things wedding before curating a design that will fit perfectly within the styling of the day.

www.studiocakeart.com.au

ALBERT TSE METALSMITH
Jewelry

We are specialising in non-traditional wedding and engagement rings at Albert Tse Metalsmith. We make all our rings uniquely one-of-a-kind because we believe that we are as unique as we are the same.

www.alberttsemetalsmith.com

BAKER BOYS BAND
Entertainment

The Baker Boys Band are live music experts and party starters, infusing every event with energy and full dance floors. Their customizable band size allows you to find the right fit for your style & budget. See them perform live!

www.bakerboysband.com.au

BMF DESIGNS
Stationery

We are lovers of love, design and beautiful stationery, creating affordable and bespoke designs for any occasion. We believe stationery sets the tone for any engagement or wedding and we understand the importance of bringing your ideas to life.

www.bmfdesigns.net

TUX COUTURE
Attire

Handcraft custom tuxedos for women, Tux Couture offer several style jackets and pants and other accompanying pieces for any body type. Each piece can be customized with a different color lining, piping, embroidered message on the inside, etc. If you can dream it, Tux Couture can make it.

www.tux-couture.com

L.A ROOTS CATERING
Catering

L.A.-based and headed by chef/owner Isaiah Seay, L.A. Roots Catering is devoted to culinary creativity, imaginative ingredients, and familiar yet fantastic flavor profiles. We believe in simple ingredients, sustainably and locally sourced, organic wherever possible.

www.larootscatering.com

EPHEMORA
Stationery

Ephemora offers unique wedding papers, customized for you from our studio in NYC. We want your wedding to dazzle. We'll help you get there with highly customizable, limited-edition designs that stand out from the crowd. Ephemora is a gender- and relationship-affirming studio. We celebrate love in all its forms.

www.ephemora.com

COJ EVENTS
Planner & Design

COJ Events, owned by wives Cathy O'Connell & Dorry Wynham, specializes in creating LGBTQIA+ Weddings that celebrate love! Destination wedding experts based in Palm Springs, CA, COJ Events create unique, creative and joy-filled events across the world.

www.cojevents.com

USA

SELVA
Florist

SELVA creates wedding and event flowers that are organic, unstructured, unique and abundant. Designs are inspired by the ever-changing seasons, using flowering branches and daffodils for spring events, lush heirloom garden roses and cafe au lait dahlias in the summer and berries and grasses in the fall and winter.

www.selvafloraldesign.com

BIXBY + PINE
Planner & Design

We're not really on earth for a long time, so it's Bixby & Pine's goal to make meaningful relationships with people & make really rad experiences through their designs and planning. If their philosophy didn't sell you, they also like tacos, margaritas, The Bachelor and graphic tanks.

www.bixbyandpine.com

WIDE EYES PAPER CO.
Stationery

Wide Eyes Paper Co. is geared towards the adventurous couple seeking a non-traditional, whimsical and creative approach to stationery. We pride ourselves in unique printing methods such as wood-engraved invitations and fully illustrated paneled stationery for the movers and the shakers, soulful kinda folk.

www.wideeyespaperco.com

JANE ALEXANDRA EVENTS
Planner & Design

Jane Alexandra Events is a boutique Wedding Planning company dedicated to creating events inspired by you! We are not here to take over your day we are here to experience it with you, guide you through the process, and help you to design an event with a timeless yet fresh aesthetic.

www.janealexandraevents.com

VOW ART
Videography

Far from your traditional wedding videographers, the VowArt team is dedicated to creating unique and indie-inspired films that speak to today's modern couples. The husband and wife duo behind the brand film and edit with artistry, carefully crafting a film that is just as special as your wedding day.

www.vowart.ie

THE TYTHE BARN
Venue

This exclusive, stylish and award-winning venue is set on a working farm! Tythe Barn was founded in 1998, both the venue and team are consistently praised for their impeccable attention to detail.

www.thetythebarn.co.uk

MUCK FLORALS
Florist

Detail-oriented – quality-oriented. The Muck Floral team get just as much joy building large-scale hanging installations as they do delicately arranging a small tabletop display, or each thoughtfully placed bloom in your bouquet.

www.muck.co.nz

GLUCK UND LICHT
Photography

Looking for a coffee addicted photographer from the north of Germany, who enjoys hanging around with wild hearted humans beings? Capturing the intimate connection between soulmates for eternity is a pretty nice thing to Gluck und Licht- no matter their gender, sexuality or color of their skin.

www.glueckundlicht.de

AROUND THE WORLD

JENNIFER SEE STUDIOS
Photography

Practicing a true documentary approach, Jennifer See Studios travels the world, collecting inspiration and capturing the faces of true love. We believe that photography is the documentation of connection; capturing a moment's quiet interaction and the genuine emotion between people.

www.jenniferseestudios.com

4 EVENTS
Videography & Photography

4events appreciate the details, intimate moments, and emotional interactions that make your day unique and deliver photographs and films that reflect your one-of-a-kind love. In Spain, or anywhere across the globe, 4events is ready to create a beautiful visual representation of your wedding day.

www.4events.es

CLAUDIA EBELING
Photography

My name is Claudia and I live in Germany. I've been shooting weddings for five years now. I'm all about capturing the in-between moments and real emotions, the loud ones and the quiet ones and I'm lucky enough to do something I love every day.

www.claudiaebeling.com

ANTIBISUAL
Photography

Antibisual looks for couples who live their wedding at 200%. It's not always about perfectly posed images, rather capturing those moments that express the most of your wedding day, the emotions and sensations of every moment.

www.antibisual.com

THE DIRECTORY

**A CURATED COLLECTION OF INCLUSIVE WEDDING VENDORS
FROM AROUND THE WORLD**

www.dancingwithher.com/directory

Vendors from top left clockwise: Jackson Grant Weddings, Imago Creative Studio, Grey Events, Rupert on Rupert

A SPECIAL THANKS

Dancing With Her couldn't exist without an incredible network of humans from around the globe who support the publication. Whether you follow along on social media, have picked up a copy at a local store or you've found us on the world wide web, we are so grateful that you are here.

This list isn't exhaustive, but it is those who directly contributed to bringing this sixth volume of Dancing With Her magazine to life- it really couldn't be without them.

ANDI & TOVAH

APRIL EVELYN PHOTOGRAPHY
www.aprilevelynphoto.wixsite.com/aprilevelyn

BROGEN JESSUP PHOTOGRAPHY
www.brogenjessup.com

CALDER PHOTOGRAPHY
www.calderphoto.com

CHASEWILD
www.chasewild.com

CORI TAYLOR PHOTOGRAPHY
www.coritaylor.com

EMILY CHELSEA JEWELRY
www.emilychelsea.com

ERIN FRASER
www.efraserphoto.com

FAIRINA CHENG
www.fairinachengjewellery.com

FOX & KIN
www.foxandkin.com

HENRY TIEU PHOTOGRAPHY
www.henry-tieu.com

KAYLA

KENZ & NICK
www.kenzandnickphoto.com

MCKENZIE BIGLIAZZI PHOTOGRAPHY
www.mckenziebigliazzi.com

RAINWATER PHOTOGRAPHY
www.rainwater-photography.com

SAMANTHA LOWE PHOTO
www.samanthalowephoto.com

LIGHTSMITH IMAGES
www.lightsmithimages.com.au

THE NOOK
www.insidethenook.com

brachparis.com

HONEYMOON

A COLLECTION OF UNIQUE HONEYMOON OPTIONS
FROM AROUND THE WORLD

When you think about the iconic beaches in Australia, there's probably one white sanded beach that stands out, Whitehaven Beach — located in the [almost always] sunny Whitsundays, on the east coast of Queensland.

Made up of 74 islands and the mainland, the Whitsundays is most known for being host to the iconic Great Barrier Reef. There is loads of things to do so you'll want to pack your sense of adventure.

If you love the outdoors and can't think of anything more perfect than cocktails in the sun while you celebrate your new relationship status, this idyllic beachside, island wonderland, is perfect for newlyweds looking for an Australian honeymoon destination.

And, although you won't find a particularly large LGBTQ+ scene here, you will find that the community celebrates diversity. There won't be a need to hide that just married PDA!

WHITSUNDAYS, AUSTRALIA

GETTING THERE

You'll need to fly to the Whitsunday via an airport in one of Australia's capital cities. A word of warning though, the flight in is known to always be a little bumpy, so don't be alarmed if this is your experience!

It is easiest to organize a transfer from the airport to your accommodation. Taxies tend to err on the more expensive side; you would expect to pay around AU$100 for a one way trip. Alternativly, hiring a car is a cheap way to get about and will allow you to get outside of the often busy tourist spots and explore.

Depending on where you choose to base yourself [Airlie Beach is the biggest town of the area and a good place to start] there is a lot that is walkable. You will probably find yourself down at the harbor most days heading out to the islands and the sea.

WHAT TO DO

Get a suntan, see the incredible reef and sip cocktails.

While Airlie Beach might be small, the area is home to some of the most incredible natural wonders - including the Great Barrier Reef. Spending a day out with a local tour company will mean you get the opportunity to snorkle with the fish and see the incredible colors of the reef. It's a natural wonder of the world, and for good reason.

Taking the opportunity to see the coast from the sky is one of those 'once-in-a-lifetime' things. With so many islands, it's hard to realise the sheer size of the place without seeing it from a seaplane or helicopter. If you're lucky, you might even spot a majestic manta ray or the whales who call the area home for the winter.

Don't forget to ask the pilot to fly over Heart Island, a natural formation of a coral reef that is shaped perfectly like a heart.

If you've always dreamt of being a pirate, or you just like boats, you can hire your own sailboat and anchor up in the ocean. If you're not a confident captain, there are opportunities to have someone more experienced take you out and leave you for a night or three. Is there anything more romantic than willingly being lost at sea with your new spouse? Just the two of you.

Also, dine out. Some of the best chefs and mixologists from around the world have found themselves in the area [for a good reason, the weather is perfect year round], you best take advantage of that! From hatted restaurants to oyster bars, incredible seaside brunch spots, and harborside seafood feasts, this place has it all!

You'll come home full, sunkissed and relaxed.

WHERE TO STAY

The Whitsundays is home to world-class resorts, including resorts on private islands. However, if they're not your style, there are plenty of other accommodation options to choose from.

Something a little cheaper - *Mirage Whitsundays*

Fancy serviced apartments right on the waterfront. You're still in close walking proximity to the center of town, although it is just far enough out of town that you feel like you're away from the hustle and bustle. Also, the pool will entice you- don't say you weren't told.

Prices start at around AU$250 per night.

Something a little more - *Hamilton Island, Palm Bungalows*

While Hamilton Island looks dreamy, it's usually reserved for those who want to spend an arm and a leg, until these bungalows popped up. These bungalows have a more 'back to nature' feel about them, and are far enough away from everyone else so you'll feel like you've got the island to yourselves.

Prices start at around AU$400 per night.

Going all out- *Bareboat*

You don't need a license [just common sense] to hire these yachts and sail the mighty seas! With a bed, kitchen and bathroom on board, this is the ultimate private honeymoon luxury. Just anchor up and have a night under the stars surrounded by the Coral Sea.

Prices start at around AU$700 per night.

WHAT TO EAT & DRINK

Funnily enough, even though this paradise is on the ocean it isn't just seafood that is incredible here- although that is pretty good!

SHUCKZ Oyster and Champagne Bar- With Australian Oysters being shucked to order and served any way you like, along with a glass of top-shelf bubbles, is there any other way to celebrate your new status as newlywed?

Mika - Brazilian BBQ sound delicious? This stuff is authentic! We'd suggest the BBQ experience to really get a hold of all the incredible flavors.

Whitsundays Sailing Club - With classic Australian pub fare adorning the menu, grab a beer and really soak up one of the best views of the coast that the Whitsundays has to offer.

THE ANNEX
Toronto, Canada

The Annex has collaborated with the neighborhood's best to make sure you get to live like a local. Don't just sleep here—live here, and discover what hospitality was always meant to be. In addition to being a boutique hotel, ther's also a variety of unique and intentionally designed spaces to host your next event.

www.theannex.com

CAN BORDOY
Palma, Spain

Can Bordoy Grand House & Garden is a luxury hotel based in Palma, Majorca's historic Old Quarter. Opened by Founder and Chairman Don Mikael Hall, alongside Managing Director Giovanni Merello, the 2,500 sqm property features a world-class spa, a secret garden, and twenty-four well-appointed suites.

www.canbordoy.com

AMERIKALINJEN
Oslo, Norway

Amerikalinjen is a hotel built for the modern-day explorer. Set in a location that is the ideal starting point for any journey in the vibrant city of Oslo. Amerikalinjen is the perfect place for personalized, anticipating and innovative service, where the art of storytelling leaves you asking for more.

www.amerikalinjen.com

HOTEL OTTILIA
Carlsberg City, Copenhagen

Stay in a luxury 4+ star boutique hotel located in the old iconic Carlsberg Brewery. Unique industrial design, and a free wine hour every day, Hotel Ottilia will leave you wishing you had book an extra night. Organic breakfast is served daily, and all the amenities you need on site.

www.brochner-hotels.dk/hotel-ottilia

ACCOMMODATION

THE BUCKLAND STUDIOS
Bright, Australia

All accommodation options at The Buckland come with the comforts of king beds with fine linen, superbly appointed kitchens and bathrooms, and sitting rooms with designer furnishings and fire hearths. Mornings begin with fully cooked breakfasts in The Buckland Breakfast Lounge, where wakefulness is merely optional.

www.thebuckland.com.au

NOTEL
Melbourne, Australia

Six vintage Airstreams architecturally redesigned sitting atop a Melbourne CBD rooftop. Not your average function space. We are NOTEL. If you're looking for traditional, go somewhere else. If you're looking for unique and fun, then hit us up for an experience like no other!

www.notelmelbourne.com.au

CASA ADELA
San Miguel De Allende, Mexico

Originally an artist's residency, Casa Adela is an elegant retreat in San Miguel De Allende. Spend your days lazing by the mineral-rich pool, soaking in the enormous bathtubs and gathering under the stars for farm-fresh fare from the cocina. When you're ready for adventure, there are plenty of options to choose from.

www.hotelcasaadela.com

my little peony

FLORAL STYLING | CARAVAN BAR | EVENT HIRE

WWW.MYLITTLEPEONY.COM.AU